REVOLUTIONARY CHALLENGES AND OPPORTUNITIES OF FINTECH

REVOLUTIONARY CHALLENGES AND OPPORTUNITIES OF FINTECH

Edited

Shweta Anand, PhD

Shalini Srivastav, PhD

Vikas Garg, PhD

Geetika Garg

AAP APPLE ACADEMIC PRESS

First edition published 2024

Apple Academic Press Inc.
1265 Goldenrod Circle, NE,
Palm Bay, FL 32905 USA
4164 Lakeshore Road, Burlington,
ON, L7L 1A4 Canada

CRC Press
2385 NW Executive Center Drive,
Suite 320, Boca Raton FL 33431
4 Park Square, Milton Park,
Abingdon, Oxon, OX14 4RN UK

Library and Archives Canada Cataloguing in Publication

Title: Revolutionary challenges and opportunities of fintech / edited by Shweta Anand, PhD, Shalini Srivastav, PhD, Vikas Garg, PhD, Geetika Garg.
Names: Anand, Shweta, editor. | Srivastav, Shalini, editor. | Garg, Vikas (Assistant director), editor. | Garg, Geetika, editor.
Description: First edition. | Includes bibliographical references and index.
Identifiers: Canadiana (print) 20230568106 | Canadiana (ebook) 20230568157 | ISBN 9781774915042 (hardcover) | ISBN 9781774915059 (softcover) | ISBN 9781003428718 (ebook)
Subjects: LCSH: Finance—Technological innovations. | LCSH: Financial services industry—Technological innovations. | LCSH: Artificial intelligence—Economic aspects.
Classification: LCC HG173 .R48 2024 | DDC 332—dc23

Library of Congress Cataloging-in-Publication Data

Names: Anand, Shweta, editor.

Title: Revolutionary challenges and opportunities of fintech / edited by Shweta Anand, PhD, Shalini Srivastav, PhD, Vikas Garg, PhD, Geetika Garg.

Description: First edition. | Palm Bay, FL : Apple Academic Press, 2024. | Includes bibliographical references and index. | Summary: "This book explores the emergence of artificial intelligence blended with financial concepts as a promising new area in business and technology-financial technology, or fintech. The book introduces the very relevant concepts of fintech, its financial derivatives, management information systems, and artificial intelligence and provides tools to find solutions to complex problems in the finance and investment domain. The case studies provide firsthand knowledge of real problems faced by the industry and highlights the thought processes in resolution of complex problems. Topics address the global adoption of fintech, fintech disruptions in the financial sector, the use of machine learning and artificial intelligence to increase the effectiveness of financial trading algorithms, fintech in retail banking and risk management, inbound marketing as well as internal marketing for fintech, fintech in the international education sector, and more. Both business professionals and those in the technical industry will find this book to be of great use. It will be quite helpful for both professionals and students in the fields of finance and artificial intelligence"-- Provided by publisher.

Identifiers: LCCN 2023050991 (print) | LCCN 2023050992 (ebook) | ISBN 9781774915042 (hardcover) | ISBN 9781774915059 (paperback) | ISBN 9781003428718 (ebook)

Subjects: LCSH: Finance--Technological innovations.

Classification: LCC HG173 .R486 2024 (print) | LCC HG173 (ebook) | DDC 332--dc23/eng/20231103

LC record available at https://lccn.loc.gov/2023050991

LC ebook record available at https://lccn.loc.gov/2023050992

ISBN: 978-1-77491-504-2 (hbk)
ISBN: 978-1-77491-505-9 (pbk)
ISBN: 978-1-00342-871-8 (ebk)

About the Editors

Shweta Anand, PhD

Shweta Anand, PhD, CMA is the former Dean of Academics, Dean of Research and Planning, Dean School of Management. She is currently Dean of School of Buddhist Studies and Civilization at Gautam Buddha University, Greater Noida, UP, India.

She is qualified in MCom, PGDM in Finance, ICWAI, and has a PhD in Wealth Management.from MNNIT Allahabad. Her PhD supervisor is Prof Peeush Ranjan Agrawal, a. renowned academician. She has more than three decades of varied experience. Currently a Professor of Practice, she started her career by serving at Indian financial institutions, moved on to more challenging and global roles in the IT sector as a financial services consultant. She thereafter entered academics in 2008 to bring in practical experience to the academic world. While in academics, she has authored several publications in high-impact journals and books. She has successfully guided several PhD researchers. She also serves on various panels, editorial and advisory boards. She has several awards and accolades to her credit.

Shalini Srivastav, PhD

Shalini Srivastav, PhD, has over 16 years of experience in teaching, research, and consultancy and almost three years of corporate experience. During these years, she has played many roles, including teacher, trainer, mentor, counsellor, and administrator. Her research areas are diverse and include financial management, financial services, investment management, project management, auditing, etc. In addition to organizing and participating in many conferences, seminars, workshops, and faculty development programs, she has published business cases and research papers in national and international journals and has been granted 14 copyrights. She is a life member of the Indian Commerce Association and the Integrated Chambers of Commerce and Industry (ICCI), New Delhi. She is also serving as a reviewer and advisory board member of various journals of international repute. She has earned awards for her research. She is a blogger and loves to write articles on finance. She has a vast global exposure, and she believes in encouraging and motivating students to face challenges by sharing with them her blend of academic and corporate experience.

Vikas Garg, PhD

Vikas Garg, PhD, is Assistant Director of the Executive Programs Management Domain at Amity University, Uttar Pradesh, India. He has an 20+ years of experience and more than 10 PhD scholars currently under his guidance. He has published numerous research papers in various Scopus- and ABDC-indexed international and national journals. He is acting as Associate Editor of the *Journal of Sustainable Finance and Investment,* (indexed in the WoS and Scopus). He is also acting as the Book Series Editor for Taylor and Francis for three books series: *Technology Innovations: Strategies for Business Sustainability and Growth; Emerging Trends in Technology in Management and Commerce;* and *Electronic Commerce Management for Business*. He has been working with new innovative ideas in the field of patents and copyrights. He has been the lead organizer in conducting various international conferences, workshops, and case study competitions, including those affiliated with IEEE. He has been conferred with many national and international awards for being best academician, researcher, and employee.

Geetika Garg, MPhil

Geetika Garg holds the degrees of MCom, MBA (Finance), and MPhil (Commerce) and has more than 15 years of experience as a finance professor at reputed institutes. Currently, she is working in the Bhai Gurdas Group of Institutions in the Commerce and Management Department, India. There, she has been working since 2016 and now she is serving as Department Chair. She formerly served as an Assistant Professor of Finance at HIMT Group of Institutions in Management Department. She is a great motivator and focuses on improvement of students' development in management and supports the teacher-learning process. Ms. Garg has a keen interest in research. During her MPhil, she prepared her thesis on the volatility of the Indian Stock Market compared with other countries' stock markets. She published many papers in both international and national conferences. She has attended many workshops and seminars, which have expanded her research areas. As a teacher in the management department, she has helped in more than 1000 MBA projects. In her current position, she is very active in conducting various events for the growth and overall development of students. Now, she is planning to pursue her doctorate in Finance to enhance and widen her research area.

Contents

Contributors

Vrinda Agarwal
Amity University, Noida Campus, Noida, Uttar Pradesh, India

Shweta Anand
School of Management, Gautam Buddha University, Greater Noida, India

Amit Kumar Arora
KIET Group of Institutions, Delhi-NCR, Ghaziabad, India

Geetika Garg
Bhai Gurdas Group of Institutions, Punjab, India

Nishtha Garg
Amity University, Noida Campus, Noida, Uttar Pradesh, India

Vikas Garg
Amity University, Greater Noida Campus, Greater Noida, Uttar Pradesh, India

Monika Goel
Institute of Research and Studies, Faridabad, India

Harshita Gupta
Department of Commerce, Delhi School of Economics, Delhi University, Delhi, India

Vijay Prakash Gupta
Institute of Business Management, GLA University, Mathura, U.P. India

Teena Hassija
Institute of Research and Studies, Faridabad, India

Amanjot Kaur
Bhai Gurdas Institute of Management and Technology, Sangrur, Punjab, India

Jasmeet Kaur
Jagan Institute of Management Studies, Sector 5, Rohini, New Delhi, India

Jyoti Kukreja
Jagannath International Management School, Kalkaji, New Delhi

Gaurav Nagpal
Birla Institute of Technology and Science, Pilani campus, Rajasthan, India

Jyotsna Oswal
Jagan Institute of Management Studies, Sector 5, Rohini, New Delhi, India

Anirudh Pandit
Bhai Gurudas Institute, Sangrur, Punjab, India

Neha Puri
Amity University, Noida Campus, Uttar Pradesh, India

Namita Rajput
Sri Aurobindo College, Delhi University, New Delhi, India

Hridyanshu Shaktawat
Birla Institute of Technology and Science, Pilani campus, Rajasthan, India

Amit Kumar Singh
Department of Commerce, Delhi School of Economics, Delhi University, India

Harjit Singh
Symbiosis Centre for Management Studies Noida, Symbiosis International University Pune, India

Harpreet Singh
Punjab Institute of Management and Technology, Alour, Khanna, India

Abhishek Sinha
Vigyan Jyoti Institute of Management, Hyderabad, India

Rohit Kumar Srivastav
Department of Commerce, Delhi School of Economics, Delhi University, India

Shalini Srivastav
Amity University, Greater Noida Campus, Greater Noida, Uttar Pradesh, India

Anita Venaik
Amity University, Noida Campus, Noida, Uttar Pradesh, India

Swati Watts
Institute of Research and Studies, Faridabad, India

Abbreviations

AAPL	Apple
AI	artificial intelligence
algo	algorithm
AMCs	asset management companies
AML	anti-money laundering
AR	augmented reality
BABA	Alibaba
B2C	business to the client
CAGR	compound annual growth rate
CAGR	cumulative aggregate gross returns
CD	coordinate descent
DDC	daily day counter
HFF 200	how far from 200 day moving average
HFF 50	how far from 50 day moving average
HFF previous high	how far from previous 52 weeks high
HFF previous low	how far from previous 52 weeks low
ICOs	initial coin offerings
KYC	know your customer
LTMA	long-term moving average or 200 day moving average
MAS	Monetary Authority of Singapore
MST	multi-spread trading
PctChg	percentage change
PPC	pay per click
RPA	robotic process automation
SEO	search engine optimization
STMA	short-term moving average or 50 day moving average
TAM	technology acceptance model
UPI	unified payment interface

Preface

The world of finance has undergone a remarkable transformation in recent years, driven by the relentless march of technology. From the early days of credit cards to the advent of online banking, and now, the rise of cryptocurrencies and decentralized finance (DeFi), the financial services industry has continually adapted to embrace innovation. This book, *Revolutionary Challenges and Opportunities of Fintech*, explores the dynamic landscape of financial technology (fintech) and its profound impact on the way we interact with money, invest, and transact.

Fintech, short for financial technology, is more than just a buzzword; it represents a fundamental shift in how financial services are conceived, delivered, and experienced. The fusion of finance and technology has unleashed a wave of innovation that promises greater convenience, accessibility, and efficiency in financial transactions and services. However, with this revolution come a host of challenges and uncertainties that demand our careful consideration.

In this book, we embark on a journey through the ever-evolving world of fintech. We delve into the historical antecedents of financial innovation, tracing the roots of fintech back to the earliest forms of currency exchange. We also examine the key drivers and catalysts that have propelled fintech into the mainstream, reshaping the traditional banking and investment landscape along the way.

Chapter 1. An Application of Action Research to a Portfolio of Investments Using Machine Learning to Increase the Effectiveness of Financial Trading Algorithms: The goal of this research project is to enhance the decision-making process in financial trading, potentially leading to better returns and reduced risks for the portfolio of investments. It also highlights the importance of combining academic research methodologies with practical applications in the financial industry.

Chapter 2. Global Adoption of Fintech: This chapter talks about global rise of Fintech due to its convenience, cost-effectiveness, innovation, and potential for financial inclusion. However, its pace and extent of adoption can vary depending on factors such as regulation, competition, trust, and demographics.

Chapter 3. Fintech Disruptions in the Financial Sector: Opportunities, Challenges, and the Future: This paper represents a significant transformation in the way financial services are delivered, consumed, and regulated. These disruptions have created both opportunities and challenges for various stakeholders, including traditional financial institutions, startups, consumers, and regulators.

Chapter 4. Fintech Retail Banking and Risk Management: Best Practices: Fintech (financial technology) has transformed the landscape of retail banking and risk management by introducing innovative solutions and best practices. Fintech retail banking and risk management best practices involve the integration of technology, data analytics, and customer-centricity to create a more efficient, secure, and personalized banking experience while effectively managing risks and complying with regulations.

Chapter 5. Challenges of Fintech Challenges and Suggested Strategies to Overcome: Fintech startups, like any other type of technology-based startup, face a unique set of challenges in their quest to disrupt and innovate within the financial industry. These challenges can vary depending on the specific niche or segment of fintech the startup is targeting, but there are some common hurdles that many fintech startups encounter.

Chapter 6. Fintech: The Financial Sector's Digital Reformation: Fintech is the digital reformation of the financial sector, driven by technological advancements and characterized by increased accessibility, innovation, efficiency, and improved user experiences. It is changing how people manage their money, access financial services, and invest, and it continues to evolve as technology advances further.

Chapter 7. Global Understanding of Fintech: Inbound marketing for fintech, like inbound marketing for any industry, is a strategy that focuses on attracting, engaging, and converting potential customers through relevant and valuable content rather than interruptive advertising. The key to effective inbound marketing for fintech is to develop a deep understanding of the fintech industry, its target audience, and its unique challenges and opportunities.

Chapter 8. Inbound Marketing for Fintech: Inbound marketing for fintech involves understanding the fintech industry, knowing your target audience, creating valuable content, optimizing for search engines and social media, generating leads, and building lasting customer relationships. By following these principles, fintech companies can effectively attract and retain customers in a highly competitive and rapidly evolving industry.

Chapter 9. Internal Marketing and Employee Motivation Builds Psychological Ownership in Fintech Emotional Intelligence in Industry 4.0: Fostering a culture of internal marketing, employee motivation, and emotional intelligence in a fintech company operating in the era of Industry 4.0 can lead to employees feeling a strong sense of psychological ownership. This, in turn, can contribute to their increased commitment, creativity, and willingness to drive the organization's success in a highly competitive and dynamic industry.

Chapter 10. Fintech: Disruption in the International Education Sector: This paper offers numerous opportunities to improve the financial aspects of international education, it's essential to address regulatory and security concerns, such as data privacy and fraud prevention, to ensure the safety and trust of students and institutions in this evolving landscape.

Chapter 11. Global Revolutionary Challenges and Opportunities of Fintech: Fintech presents both revolutionary challenges and opportunities on a global scale. While it disrupts traditional financial systems and poses regulatory and security challenges, it also has the potential to drive financial inclusion, boost efficiency, spur innovation, and improve access to financial services worldwide. Managing these challenges while harnessing the opportunities will be crucial for the continued growth and development of the fintech industry.

Chapter 12. Major Challenges and Benefits of Fintech Across the Globe: Fintech has brought about numerous benefits by improving access to financial services, enhancing convenience, reducing costs, and driving innovation. However, it also faces challenges related to security, regulation, trust, data privacy, competition, and financial stability. The continued growth and success of the fintech industry depend on addressing these challenges while harnessing its transformative potential.

The book also investigates the role of fintech in financial inclusion, sustainability, and the global economy. We consider how emerging technologies like blockchain and artificial intelligence are reshaping the way we think about currency, payments, and asset management. Additionally, we examine the regulatory landscape that governs fintech, as governments and institutions grapple with the need to strike a balance between innovation and oversight.

As we traverse these topics, we aim to provide a comprehensive overview of the multifaceted world of fintech. This book is designed for readers from all walks of life, whether you are a seasoned financial professional seeking insights into the latest trends or an individual looking to better understand the fintech products and services that are becoming increasingly integrated into everyday life.

CHAPTER 1

Application of Action Research to a Portfolio of Investments Using Machine Learning to Increase the Effectiveness of Financial Trading Algorithms

HRIDYANSHU SHAKTAWAT and GAURAV NAGPAL

Birla Institute of Technology and Science, Pilani campus, Rajasthan, India

ABSTRACT

This article describes the action research executed to improve the efficiency of trading algorithms in the stock markets. The outcomes of the stock market are predicted using fundamental algorithms. This study is about how to incorporate machine learning in such algorithms, and how to make them more productive so that the final portfolio values are increased and less volatile. The paper also pens down the benefits achieved by this exercise in terms of reduced volatility of returns, lesser drawdown, and improved sharp ratio. The different machine learning rules are applied to the base algorithm, and their performance on the virtual portfolios thus created, is determined. Some heuristics are developed on whether to follow the signal given by the base algorithm or make the flipped decision or stay neutral on going for long and short decisions. The rules are based on the decision trees, logistic regression, k nearest neighbor, and Gaussian Naïve method.

Revolutionary Challenges and Opportunities of Fintech. Shweta Anand, PhD, Shalini Srivastav, PhD, Vikas Garg, PhD, & Geetika Garg (Eds.)

1.1 INTRODUCTION

This is the action research done in an organization that has been advising for decades a stock market investor on how to invest in a wise manner to get good and liable returns. It's a product-based company it makes different products based on data analysis and research of the stock market. It has a Market equity research team that works on generating signals about different stocks whether to buy them, sell them, or short sell all. The organization also has a "Data Science" team which on which the equity research team is dependent to analyze the data and apply different algorithms to predict the stock market. In order for the machine to forecast outcomes and provide us with favorable results on our portfolio, the company must apply all the new rules as well as some outdated thumb rules utilized by stock brokers. It continuously creates new algorithms and attempts to implement them in active markets to gauge their effectiveness. The outcomes of the stock market are predicted using fundamental algorithms.

1.2 UNDERSTANDING OF INVESTMENT PORTFOLIO

There are various trading algorithms are available nowadays in the market with most of the different companies having their own. Some of these algorithms are rule based and some of them are based on machine learning and artificial intelligence (AI) models.

Malik (2017) proposed a methodology to develop the trading algorithms, named Pattern–Insight–Model–Strategies–Trading algorithms (PIMSTA). He advised that a generic approach to design trading algorithms of all types (cryptocurrency, shares, stock market in different countries) is a bottom–up approach followed in the same sequence as PIMSTA spelled. His way of developing algorithms includes rule-based systems with stochastic approaches (standard deviation, mean variance, etc.).

Blyth (2018) showed that although the machine learning models are useful in various fields and can be implemented on the trading platform but they are only good on short-term basis and not producing efficient results on the long-term basis. Wang and Thomas (2018) showed how irrational human behavior deviates from certain ideal ideologies. So, if we try to involve machine learning and deep learning, we can get somewhat more efficient results.

Podobas (2019) formulated new formula for alternative support and resistance level using linear regression and also incorporated only one machine learning model. Bogliardi et al. (2019) introduced the concept of "Multi Spread Trading (MST)." The MST is a financial approach that does not rely on whether the market is bullish or bearish. Instead, it is based on quantitative algorithms that determine the periodic out in between three or more correlated and co-integrated assets in comparison to their statistical relative trend, making use of their inherent ability to recover to "normal" values. However, they also did not include some rule-based algorithms here. Nor did they go for machine learning optimization.

Chakraborty (2019) showed how an intelligent system based on reinforcement learning can benefit from classical financial indicators to overcome classic trading strategies in the stock market. Therefore, he used reinforcement learning on the buy signal and classic trading strategies for the sell signal. But in none of the cases did he try to combine them.

A large number of researchers are developing and analyzing machine learning techniques, fitting strategy parameters, and optimization specificity. The performance of a strategy is sensitive to even small changes in the parameters, and there are many local extrema that are unevenly distributed throughout the solution space. The techniques are intended to significantly reduce computing time while maintaining a high level of strategy quality. In the case of a moving averages crossover system, the effectiveness of various strategies is often contrasted for three different pairs of assets. Although there is work on improvising trading algorithms using machine learning but they do not include various machine learning models. Nor do they optimize the final output the way this study does.

A large number of researchers are developing and analyzing machine learning techniques, fitting strategy parameters, and optimization specificity. The performance of a strategy is sensitive to even small changes in the parameters, and there are many local extreme situations that are unevenly distributed throughout the solution space. The techniques are intended to significantly reduce computing time while maintaining a high level of strategy quality. In the case of a moving averages crossover system, the effectiveness of various strategies is often contrasted for three different pairs of assets.

1.3 METHODOLOGY

This research study is done on one such algorithm to convert it first into Python code and then to enhance its performance by using machine learning techniques. To begin with, an excel sheet containing the rules was converted into the Python code so that we can find the sensitivity of some variables which we are using in the stock market's forecasting. This is necessary to invest judicially in the stock market to earn good returns. This algorithm deals with some of the thumb rules in stock marketing with the rules. In this algorithm, we have to predict the investment level. Investment level is the percentage of the amount of your cash that you want to invest in the market this investment level has to be designed based on the previous market conditions. Then after calculating the investment level, we have to calculate the portfolio of that which includes the calculation of share trades, commission, etc.

So, it is an overall rule-based algorithm each rule depends upon some other rule's outcomes. In this algorithm, while developing it, NQDC (American stock market like NIFTY of India) data was used. Also used were some standard inputs such as volume of trades, open price, close price, and high and low of the day. These all things are easily collected from NQDC.

After collecting raw data, some operations were performed on it to make it meaningful data. For example, from the closing market, the authors calculated the 50 days moving average, 200 days moving average, percentage change, returns, previous high and low in a back window, and many more such ratios. After calculating those ratios, the rules were calculated. The beauty in the calculation of those rules is that each and every rule depends upon some other rule's results.

So, while devising those rules, one needs to be careful of their sequence and call in Python there are about 56 rules and some variables involved in the calculation of those rules. After all the rules were made, the investment level (called as weight here) was computed. After the calculation of the investment level, the portfolio value was determined. With the help of the results of Portfolio we can decide whether the results are good or not, what is the CAGR (cumulative aggregate gross returns), short ratio, drawdown, etc.?

Now, the machine learning techniques were applied to the above-mentioned algorithm to make it deliver lesser volatile returns. We decided to use a logistic regression model to predict the investment level of without using those rules of the base model. A machine learning model with features (the ratios which can be created from the raw data such as, short-term moving average, long-term moving average, previous high, previous low, how far from the previous low, how far from previous high, percentage change, returns, volume and day down counter) was created. As a label, the investment level (weight) was chosen; it has three values 1 (the market is long or in the rally), −1 (short selling must market about to fall), and 0 (out of the market).

Logistic regression is used as a multinomial classification model with a solver as sag and a maximum iteration of 1000. It gave us about 91.8% accuracy but the portfolio returns were reduced from 399,758 to 44,353 only and the maximum drawdown decreased from 28.3% to 26%. Since the overall calmer ratio was too low as compared to the original model, we could not proceed with this model alone. Since the logistic regression was not giving the proper result, the data was trained using dynamic training data set. The data set was trained on the rolling window while appending a new entry and dropping the oldest one. This improved the performance by increasing the results from 44,353 to 150,000 but still, it is less than the base model. Volatility is also increased.

Now, it was decided to predict whether the results of the above-stated model are right or not, that is, whether those results are going to be true or false. This time we have labeled it as an accuracy that has two values 1 and −1. Features are the same as before that we used for the calculation of weights. We predicted the accuracy of the results of the above-mentioned algo in binary form as either true or false. For the prediction of accuracy, we used four different models of machine learning to get the results. These all models are coming under the category of machine learning classifiers. We used the classifier algorithm because we have a randomly distributed data set. It contains only binary classification and huge data from which classification can be done properly.

1.3.1 LOGISTIC REGRESSION

In this model, the same features were used, as used in the prediction of weights earlier but the label used was accuracy. The solver used was “sag.” Prediction output was 1 or −1.

1.3.1.1 DECISION TREE

The same features were used as in the logistic regression model, but the label used was the accuracy. This model was created on three different depths of 1, 3, and 5. And the results of three different depths were stored.

1.3.1.2 KNN (K-NEAREST NEIGHBORS)

In this model also, the features and labels used are the same as in the above two models. However, this model was developed for three different neighbors $n = (1, 3, 5)$. Every result of prediction was stored for all these different n.

1.3.2 GAUSSIAN NAIVE

In this model also features and labels are the same and predicted results are 1 or −1. 1 as true of accuracy and −1 as false of accuracy.

Now after getting all the results, they were assembled in separate files, and some rules were used after observing the patterns, which are mentioned in the following.

1.3.2.1 RULES AND OUTCOMES

Rule 1:
If all four different classification models with their different depths (for decision tree) and neighbors (for knn) give the same result for weight, then we take that into consideration otherwise we do not. So, a separate column was created in the XL and the accuracy value either was taken as 1 or −1 or 0.

Rule 2:
In this rule, we take the values of the accuracy as predicted by the models only when logistic regression is = gaussian newton = any one of the decision tree models means either with the depth of (1 or 3 or 5) = any one of the knn models means either with $n = (1 \text{ or } 3 \text{ or } 5)$.

Rule 3:

In this rule, we separately calculate the probability of each model. After calculating the probabilities, we normalize them so that the total sum of the probabilities of all the model remains 1. Now, we multiply those probabilities by the prediction probabilities of those models toward predicting the accuracy of the base algorithm; and then, multiply that with the predicted values of the accuracy of each model and then, we sum them up among all the models this summed up values range is −1 to 1.

After building up the machine learning models, predicting the results, and calculating those rules based on my observation, the following exercise was done:

The prediction accuracy value was determined using Rule 1. If it is 1, we decide to invest more than 100% because we are sure of generating good returns, and can take the risk.

For the prediction of −1 in Rule 1, we use Rule 2 and Rule 3. If the value of Rule 2 is −1 and Rule 3 is < -0.7 then we flip the investment level of the base algorithm from 100 to −100% or from −100 to 100%. Because this time, we are sure that the algorithm will give the wrong results.

If both of the above-mentioned situations are not compatible, then we decide to go with the original base algo values because in that scenario we cannot be sure of the right decision using machine learning.

1.4 OUTCOMES

- CAGR has increased by 11.59%, from 27.5% (base model) to 39.09%.
- Maximum drawdown has decreased by 6.38% from 28.58% (base-model) to 22.96%.
- Average drawdown has also decreased by 3.62% from 6.16% (base model) to 3.78%.

These results are quite good because the algorithm is having already good performance and still we can able to modify it.

To show that our models are predicting the correct points when the algorithm is about to predict wrong. Instead of flipping the investment level from long to short and short to long, we have flipped by 1000 times extra so that we can able to see that wherever we are actually predicting rightly or incorrectly prediction of our algo and modifies it.

1.5 CONCLUSION

We can see that a model grounded in logic and specific principles can produce far more reliable outcomes. We may rely on it, make smart stock market investments, and see positive outcomes, much like a foundational algorithm does in the stock market. We can take different actions depending on previous trends and make more accurate predictions by using that algorithm in Python code. We can observe that the machine learning models can really develop a rule-based system that is more productive. However, we need to note that only using the machine learning model on the raw data cannot give us good results. It is not productive to just train the machine on the raw data and try to predict tomorrow on the basis of that training. This is so because the stock market works on human emotions and market conditions, and there can be a billion combinations that can exist for one result. That is why the data is too scattered and volatile. Because of this volatility, we can't go ahead with developing directly a machine learning algorithm. Instead, if we combine a rule-based system with the machine learning model, it gives us good results. We also cannot go simply with only one model because of the diversity of classification. Rather, we will get more accurate results when we apply different models, analyze them and then apply rules to them resulting in good results.

1.5.1 A FEW POINTS OF CAUTION TO BE EXERCISED

(1) To avoid the forward biases while designing the ML models because a lot of features that people think are important contain the information of future that you will never have, so you just be aware of this while choosing your features, For example, you may take investment level that your algorithm gives as a feature to train the model but your model is calculating that on the basis of previous market conditions because your model has to predict the next day, so while training you have to shift your investment level one up and again while using them in you model you have to shift them one down.

(2) The ML and AI models require data which are balanced, in stock market conditions balancing of data is not always possible but still sometimes for balancing we create false database; this thing should be avoided while doing on stock market data because by doing so you eliminate the originality of volatility of the stock market and biases which is there in human thinking responsible of such behavior market which should be learned by the ML and AI.
(3) Since AI and ML have taken off a big part of our workloads in other domains, this can also become commonplace in equity research soon. The diffusion of such models will require the integration of the trading terminals with the AI ML tools, higher AI literacy among equity researchers, and higher processing speeds of the computational infrastructure used for financial trading.
(4) An important caution is that the overdependence on these tools does not make the existing intellectual capital of the Financial World mere consumers of the insights but leads them to the development of furthermore sophisticated insights and systems that can help generate even better returns for the shareholders.

APPENDIX

MARKET CONDITIONS

- RALLY = 0
- CORRECTION = 0.25
- UNDER PRESSURE = 0.5
- RALLY ATTEMPT = 1
- Number is just to make a character to numeric values so that we can feed in training data set in the machine learning model

Base model characteristics
- CAGR = 27.5%
- Maximum drawdown = 28.58%
- Average drawdown = 6.16%
- Time(on which model is tested) = 18 years
- Initial investment = $5000
- After 18 years portfolio became = $397,758

LOGISTIC REGRESSION:

- Used as a binomial Classifier
- From sklearn.linear_model import LogisticRegression
- Slover = “sag”
- Maximum iterations = 1000 Different solvers in Logistic Regression: Newton cg, sag, lbfgs, liblinear
- Newton cg:
    - o Newton’s method uses in a sense a better quadratic function minimization. A better because it uses the quadratic approximation
- Sag:
    - o This solver is used for sparse multinomial logistic regression and it is also suitable for very large datasets.
- L-BFGS:
    - o L-BFGS relatively performs the best compared to other methods especially it saves a lot of memory
- Liblinear:
    - o The solver uses a coordinate descent (CD) algorithm that solves optimization problems by successively performing approximate minimization along coordinate directions or coordinate hyperplanes.

K NEAREST NEIGHBOR:

- Used as binomial classifier
- Three different *n* values used: = (1, 3, 5)
- *N* = 5 is the best hit rate among all

GAUSSIAN NAIVE:

- Used as binomial classifier
- All fields are taken as default values

DECISION TREE:

- Used as a binomial classifier
- Three depths have been used = (3, 5, 7)
- Percentage correct predictions are most when depth is 7
- sklearn.tree import Decision Tree Classifier

MULTILAYER PERCEPTRON:

- It contains three hidden layers
- Neurons are:
    - o 18, 12, 6, 1 on respective layers

- activation function for the last layer is sigmoidal
- Loss is considered as " binary cross entropy"
- Optimizer used is "adam"

KEYWORDS

- **artificial intelligence**
- **financial trading algorithm**
- **decision tree**
- **Gaussian Naïve theory**
- **investment level**
- **prediction accuracy**
- **logistic regression**
- ***k* nearest neighbor**

REFERENCES

Blyth, S. Big Data and Machine Learning Won't Save Us from Another Financial Crisis, 2018. https://hbr.org/2018/09/big-data-and-machine-learning-wont-save-us-from-another-financial-crisis

Bogliardi, M.; Canepa, F. S.; Frisina, G. Multi Spread Trading—An Investment Methodology Neutral to Financial Market Trends 2019. DOI: 10.13140/RG.2.2.26691.86567.

Chakraborty, S. Deep Reinforcement Learning in Financial Markets, 2019. https://www.researchgate.net/publication/334388608_Deep_Reinforcement_Learning_in_Financial_Markets

Malik, S. PIMSTA: A Proposed Bottom-Up Layered Approach to Designing Trading Algorithms, 2017. https://www.academia.edu/38114991/Title_PIMSTA_a_proposed_bottom-up_layered_approach_to_designing_trading_algorithms

Podobas, W. J. Modelling the Alternative Support and Resistance Levels with the Application of the Linear Regression, 2019. https://www.academia.edu/39724698/Modelling_the_alternative support_and_resistance_levels_with_the_application_of_the_linear_regression

Wang, C. C. Y.; Thomas, K. New Constructs: Disrupting Fundamental Analysis with Robo-Analysts, 2018. https://store.hbr.org/product/new-constructs-disrupting-fundamental-analysis-with-robo-analysts/118068

CHAPTER 2

Global Adoption of Fintech

NAMITA RAJPUT[1], VIKAS GARG[2], JASMEET KAUR[3], and JYOTSNA OSWAL[3]

[1]*Sri Aurobindo College, Delhi University, New Delhi, India*

[2]*Amity University, Greater Noida Campus, Uttar Pradesh, India*

[3]*Jagan Institute of Management Studies, Sector-5, Rohini, New Delhi, India*

ABSTRACT

In this chapter, we have discussed FinTech technology and its adoption worldwide by customers who want to deal with their lives through the digital platform, including financial and banking services, the proportion of utilization is exemplary in every country. The idea behind this study is to make people understand the concept of FinTech, a breakthrough in the financial field. In reality, the level of adoption is different in various geographical areas. Some studies have attempted to clarify the motivation behind the global adoption of this technology. Thus, the usefulness of this chapter is to present a review of the advancement and utilization of financial technologies, as a plan of action, and to feature how FinTech adds to improving economic and social conditions, facilitating the financial services using the digital platform.

FinTech is financial innovation; FinTech offers a wide range of banking and non-banking financial services. FinTech organizations are also collaborating with banking institutions for digital financial services

Revolutionary Challenges and Opportunities of Fintech. Shweta Anand, PhD, Shalini Srivastav, PhD, Vikas Garg, PhD, & Geetika Garg (Eds.)

thus leading to more secure transactions occurring in real-time. The advantages of FinTech services at lesser cost and efficiency in operations. Thus, developed and emerging nations have different levels of FinTech adoption ensuring the global acceptance of innovations.

2.1 ABOUT FINTECH

The word FinTech is coined after "financial technology." The term FinTech consists of an extensive range of services, technologies, software, and business models that aim at advancing the financial services sector. It includes everything from cashless payments, crowdfunding platforms, Robo advisory, and virtual currencies like bitcoin. FinTech is transforming how we borrow and make payments. Since 2010, the FinTech industry has seen an increase in global investment of around $100 billion. Fintech investment increased by 18% in 2017 alone. The majority of the funding went to startups with a focus on payment and binding technologies. With Apple Pay and Ali Pay, some of the biggest corporations, including Alibaba and Apple, are investing heavily in it. In the top 20 economies, one in three people claims to have used at least two FinTech services in the previous six months. With a sizable consumer base using financial services including money transfers, financial planning, loans, and insurance, China and India are leading the way.

For people without access to traditional banking services around the world, financial technology has filled a need. Nearly 2 billion individuals worldwide are thought to lack bank accounts. Traditional bankers, insurers, and asset managers have been compelled to adopt cutting-edge digital technologies through the usage of FinTech. Institutions that provide financial services offer a variety of services on a single platform. These services' range of offerings includes everything from traditional banking services to mortgage and trading services. In other words, FinTech separates these services into offerings for a specific person. FinTech companies can operate more efficiently and cut down on transaction costs by combining services catered to individual needs with technology.

For instance, computerized financial planning services called Robo advising services are becoming a requirement for asset managers. These services can be cheaper than traditional asset managers and are accessible around the clock. FinTech is revolutionizing how we borrow money and send money. Global investment in the FinTech sector has increased by almost $100 billion since 2010. Investment in FinTech rose by 18% alone in 2017. Startups that were primarily interested in payment and binding technology received the majority of the investment. Some of the largest companies, like Alibaba and Apple, are making significant investments in Apple Pay and Ali Pay. One in three people claims to have used at least two FinTech services in the preceding 6 months in the top 20 economies.

China and India are setting the standard for FinTech with a big customer base that uses financial services like money transfers, financial planning, loans, and insurance; all a person needs is a phone to take out a loan or insurance, etc. These services might not be required to set aside as much money in case consumers default on their loans as traditional banking does because peer-to-peer lending platforms, an example, allow individuals to borrow and lend without going through banks.

With the rise of the 21st century, this technology was initially deployed on the back-end systems of various financial institutions. A recent (Parameshwar et al., 2019) study focused on how the disruptions from FinTech have transformed the way traditional banking operates and how adoption leads to influence the growth in the South Asian region considering the factors such as gross domestic product (GDP) and investment in FinTech organizations. It has stated that savings are impacted due to the change in the system through Internet banking.

Since then, its applications are extending to other sectors such as education, healthcare, wealth management, supply chain management, banking, etc. Like any growing industry, FinTech is not without risk and government regulators have struggled to control the risks associated with the rapid pace of innovation.

As FinTech allows customers the ease of access to the personal financial database, mobile banking, and investment opportunities in contemporary ways, there is vulnerability to frauds, hacking attempts, etc. because this is a platform where there is joint interaction of the software with traditional banking systems. This problem arises due to a lack of uniform regulatory frameworks. Also, it is studied (Saksonova and Kuzmina-Merlino, 2017) that due to unawareness about FinTech and continuing traditional banking practices in a country such as Latvia, the major concern is a lack of well-informed consumers. Numerous banking institutions enter a contract with FinTech organizations to enhance interface functionality or look over

FinTechs as industry competitors. With this, both banking institutions and FinTechs spurred quick innovations unmatched by developments in the government's regulatory landscape. As more firms go digital, these issues affecting financial technology are expected to get worse. So, the FinTech industry is at a crossroads regarding data privacy, security, and regulatory frameworks.

2.2 FINTECH EVOLUTION

FinTech is a platform where financial services and technology collide. The phenomenon is in existence since the 1800s when banks and financial institutions were the early adopters of new technological innovations. The evolution of FinTech services is described by categorizing it into three ages (Forbes, 2016).

- FinTech 1.0 (1866–1967): This era started from the innovation of the transatlantic cable to the creation of the automated teller machine (ATM), showing the potential of finance and technology can together lead to the era of financial globalization. Technological innovations, for example, the telegraph have strengthened cross-border financial linkages, enabling rapid transmission of financial information, transactions, etc.
- FinTech 2.0 (1967–2008): During this period, technology innovation was controlled by the traditional regulatory frameworks of financial services. This phase noticed the inception of electronic transfers and clearing systems, ATMs, and Internet banking. During the period of the mid-1990s, the financial services sector held the position of the only primary purchaser of IT services.
- FinTech 3.0 (from 2008 to today): With the growing integration between countries and following the serious change due to the international crisis in 2008, disruptive startups and existing technology companies have started to provide financial services through (business to business) B2B and (business to client) B2C platforms, and where newcomers in this industry try to aim at a single-purpose solution, their goal is to provide an improved experience with every single product or service.

Moreover, it is observed that banks and financial institutions are not facing competition from incumbent rivals but from those FinTechs who are persistently trying to find improved ways to deliver financial services by using sophisticated technologies. In countries where there is a lack of established financial infrastructure, rather than reimagining banking, a lot of FinTech services have to build essential infrastructure. The growth of the FinTech market across the globe is dependent on several economic and technological factors that influence entrepreneurs to start ventures for reinvention (Haddad and Hornuf, 2016). It is presented in a study that well-developed countries witness more FinTech startups and the availability of venture capital.

2.3 FINTECH USERS

FinTech companies persistently strengthen financial services to be more reachable to various businesses and consumers. By developing applications that enable financial systems easier to access and more conveniently available, businesses and people are making changes in their respective areas. Many researchers studied the factors influencing the adoption of financial services by constructing user adoption models for financial services. In a study, Hu et al. (2019), proposed an improved technology acceptance model (TAM) built using four influencing factors namely innovativeness, Government support, brand image, and risk associated as determinants to find how users adopt financial services. From the data analyzed through surveys, it is revealed that "Trust" in FinTech is an important factor influencing the user's attitudes toward adoption.

Over the years, however, there is rapid FinTech development. Keeping it in view, this accelerated growth is the generation of opportunities for all FinTech users to interact with each uninterruptedly. Developments towards the decentralization of access, accuracy in analytics, big data, AI, and mobile banking will be key.

There are two common, function-centric FinTech user categories and these are as follows:

- B2B for banks
- Bank's business clients

- B2C for small businesses
- Customers

The majority of the banking industry's transition to FinTech concentrated on B2C applications like lending and payment services. Prior to the development of FinTech, firms had to apply for loans at banks. Companies can now readily access loans and financial services thanks to the potential FinTech applications. Beyond banks, B2B businesses are expanding thanks to ongoing technological advancements, and they may readily access finance and other financial services. With the help of modern FinTech B2B services, FinTechs may take full use of their financial transactions to increase productivity and total profits.

FinTech provides many B2C services by the way of developing mobile phone applications such as PayPal, Apple Pay, Google Pay, PayTm, etc.

This allows people to transfer money via mobile applications simultaneously over the Internet. This innovation has made complex transaction processes easier which were traditionally not possible by a single click. Today, FinTech presents a wide range of B2C applications.

Smart money applications enable easy transfer of money to individuals sitting at different parts of the world just using a smartphone. Similar to other technological developments, the most active FinTech users are the millennials. Nowadays, as the group of millennial users is large, innovations are introduced to understand the needs of this customer base, considering their increasing purchasing power and market size. Also, Baby boomers and GenX are not that long way behind in terms of market dissemination. These two segments continue to keep on high FinTech usage rates. This is due to the fact they have a better experience of the extensive advantages of FinTechover traditional financial systems.

2.4 THE MOTIVATION BEHIND ADOPTION IN FINTECH

Financial technologies are quickly turning into an important part of the international financial system, but the magnitude of FinTech adoption within countries varies considerably. Leading research shows that factors such as unmet demand for financial services, geography, acceptability, awareness, and demographics can better explain the differences in the level of adoption.

Scaling is a significant factor considered for any startup, and FinTechs no exception. It is known that startups often face lesser roadblocks to expansion than those of established companies, that cannot maneuvers as quickly. For a FinTech startup, the set of challenges is different in the financial service sector. For expansion purposes, it is quite easy for startups to expand overseas.

Most of the FinTech do not need any physical premises rather they operate entirely online. So, the model developed digitally reduces the actual cost of expansion. In the era of big data and Machine learning, FinTechs enhances its working by scaling up thus fostering the decision-making process. This puts them in a better position than competitors who are unable to the maximum advantage of these innovations. As the FinTech innovation is exploring its potential in the financial sector, the regulators are still not able to catch up with the legal aspects. This provides an advantage to FinTech and thus they tend to develop faster than the regulators to keep up with these innovations. Similarly, FinTech companies are at advantage over those established banks and attract major investments from Venture Capital as investors presume that some of these companies may enjoy major growth in the future due to increasing demand of FinTech products by various businesses, and institutions. Different countries use a range of financial technologies to support businesses. As an example, credit systems have now scaled up economically in the USA and the UK.

However, in upcoming and developing economies like India and Bangladesh, there is a rise in mobile payments. China has made considerable progress in providing credit based on FinTech and Mobile payments. At the same time as the FinTech marketplace is probably large in developed nations, thus has more significance in these economies as it serves a huge population without the intermediary, that is, banks.

The driving force behind the FinTech adoption is to capture the market where the demand for financial services remains unserved and Mobile payments made it easy to access fundamental banking services. It has made things easier by way of making cross-border transfers of remittances relatively cheaper (Alexander, 2020).

FinTech has major changes for the economy and the growth of the economy as it could pace up financial inclusion in less-developed and emerging economies, addresses market failures, and improves and revolutionize cross-border financial integration. Some of the motivators for adopting financial technology areas as follows:

- Ease of setting up a business
- being able to offer a variety of products and services while entering the market
- World-class service chains
- Lesser cost
- 24/7 access to services
- Availability of customer-centric financial services while compared to service provided by traditional financial institutions

2.5 FINTECH INDUSTRY SEGMENTS

FinTech would create value for businesses (Leong and Sung, 2018). The idea about value creation lies in the division of FinTech applications into different categories. Globally, most of the FinTech organizations are segmented into eight broad categories namely payments, blockchain, Insurance, Planning, Trading & investments, Data and analysis, Crowdfunding, and Security (Fig. 2.1). This global FinTech landscape consists of all the sectors it is dealing into. Primarily, FinTechs are revolutionizing the process of financing or lending. Nowadays, individuals need not visit banks to carry out any financial transactions. Many FinTech companies are providing loans directly to consumers in a time frame of less than a day. Financing is further categorized into two parts: Crowdfunding and Credit & Factoring. Crowdfunding is a platform where a large number of people together raise a small number of funds for funding a project or venture with the use of the Internet. It is a form of alternative finance (Priya and Anusha, 2019).

Similarly, to lending, factoring can also be done through the internet. Presently, it is a leading alternative to get access to working capital for small business entrepreneurs with just a click of a mouse. With a simple click, companies can sell the bill receivables and get money in their accounts within a limited period without any delay. Another segment of the industry comprises "payments." Companies dealing in this segment allow people to transfer money to other people without relying on banks. Banks are imposing huge charges to make payments like peer-to-peer transfers. Also, another dimension is that the banking and financing industry was disrupted through blockchain technology introduced by FinTech companies in financial services. Presently, blockchain is used to enter smart contracts and also to record transactions as a shared digital ledger. The information stored in the decentralized ledger is difficult to steal and secured using algorithms. The data can only be shared through nodes connected. So, the biggest concern of security is being solved by blockchain technology. It is more affordable and assists in making quick payments. Third-party intermediaries like banks are no longer required. The financial industry segment includes providing advisory services.

As a part of asset management, financial and investment advisory services are planned according to the requirements of high-net-worth individuals. Customers can directly consult the wealth managers and accordingly plan their financial instruments like insurance, retirement, portfolio management, etc. An individual does not need to seek advice from different firms. The insurance market was also been major segment concentrated by the financial technology companies. These FinTechs target to reach customers through different applications. Unlike traditional insurance service providers, these are flexible. The FinTech firms are collaborating with traditional insurance service providers as the insurance sector is highly regulated.

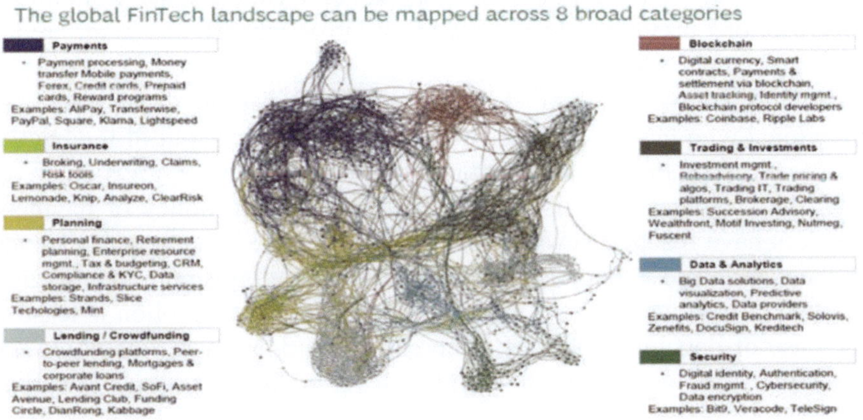

FIGURE 2.1 The global FinTech landscape can be mapped across eight broad categories.

Source: Quid, BCG/Expand/BCG Digital Venture/B Capital analysis

FinTech organizations are changing over financing or credit-advancing strategies. Individuals nowadays need not visit banks for withdrawing cash anymore. Many credit agencies presently advancing loans to clients without waiting for hours of delay in the documentation. They can scan for credits score online and get them acknowledged. Firms confirm the account holders' credit position and provide the loan. As there is a surge in FinTech lending, it is suggested that technology adoption in this area will further appreciate financial stability by granting more resilient loans (Pierri and Timmer, 2020).

2.6 WORLDWIDE TRENDS

Although the degree of adoption of FinTech services increased exponentially between 2015 and 2019, Canada and the USA have lower adoption rates than other industrialized countries. FinTech adoption has increased by a factor of two from 2015, going from 16% to 64% in 2019 (Global FinTech Adoption Index, 2019). The increased awareness of FinTech in the recent years and its sophisticated applications suggest that traditional financial services may soon become obsolete.

The growth phase of FinTech initiating from startups to expanding global offering a broad range of financial services, consumers find these organizations promising to hold funds, enable transactions, grant credit, and offer advice.

In this study, the term "FinTech adopter" is used to represent an individual who has used two or more FinTech services out of the bucket of a total of 19 services under the umbrella of FinTech innovation. With this, the awareness and use of FinTech transferring money or payment services have reached new heights reaching approximately 96%. Trends in the market show that the greatest level of adoption is seen in emerging markets, China and India (87%) whereas the level of adoption is least in the case of developed nations, such as Japan (34%) and France (35%). From this, it is evident that the adoption level in different countries varies.

2.7 UK

The UK's leading worldwide FinTech sector is empowering resilience at a time when there is uncertainty in the industry about adopting innovations, partnerships, and startups due to the outbreak of pandemic COVID-19. According to the reports (The Global City, 2020), 'UK's idea behind the adoption of FinTech is unique as it possesses worldwide expertise, a regulatory framework, access to capital, and positivity towards developing an innovative financial system. This kind of environment put the UK at a competitive advantage in such a cut-throat global competitive environment.

The importance of FinTech has proved to be more than just a subsector in the UK. The financial sector of the UK is embraced by FinTech. The benefits of FinTech are customer-centric and efficient, thus growing the network of global customers and thus bridging the gap between what customers want and how an organization can fulfill the unmet demand.

Also, accelerating FinTech investment is more than any other European country in 2018, with a record of investment through venture capital and private equity investments amounting to $3.3 billion, which is far more than Germany ($716 billion) and Switzerland ($328 billion). The graph for the investment is upward sloping with an 18% increase year on year. The UK, with the world's biggest cluster of financial and professional services providers, offers an unmatched open door for development. Also, London is considered as "excellent" for most access to FinTech clients, with an adoption rate of almost 71% which is higher among all developed economies. It can also be seen that an 82% increase in FinTech partnerships in the upcoming 3–5 years.

2.8 USA

The USA has a long history of encouraging innovations. In the USA, there is a steady increase in FinTech adoption rate over the past six years from 17 to 33% and currently only 46%. This includes the use of financial services mainly money transfer and payments, more specifically, peer-to-peer payments and non-bank transfer of money. The economic era (FinTech) revolution is a global movement to bring traditional banking financial services into a new age.

The economy of USA is nicely-positioned to hold its repute as a global FinTech leader given the country's range of economic services, skilled team of workers, and access to capital for growing and commercializing innovations, services, and products. For FinTech businesses' first expansion to America, the opportunities to discover partnership, collaboration, funding, and customers are endless. The USA has a number of the world's largest and the most valuable financial industries along with industrial banking, lending, securities change, wealth control, and insurance. Some of the notable trends are seen as follows:

- The increased use of digital delivery networks as the foremost means of providing financial products and services.
- The introduction of a cluster of services that facilitates person-to-person and consumer-to-business electronic payment systems.
- The extensive availability of markets where businesses and customers interact and promote credits.
- The inventive way of pricing automobile insurance by monitoring of driving habits using electronic devices.
- Ease of financial account aggregation and investment analysis through an online provider of financial services; and
- Fundraising through FinTech strategies such as crowdfunding and initial coin offerings (ICOs).

2.9 SOUTH AFRICA

South Africa has relatively small than other countries but an ever-growing FinTech industry with prospects of significant benefits and risks. South Africa's financial service sector has been internationally known as the world-class FinTech industry out of which three FinTechs have been listed in the "FinTech 100" list in 2016. More than 200 FinTechs are operational in South Africa till May 2019. With the trends, it is seen that some FinTechs are operational in more than one segment and segmentation of FinTech services areas:

- B2B Tech support (20%)
- Payments (30%)
- Lending (12%)
- Savings and deposits (6%)
- Insurtech (9%)
- Investments (10%)
- Financial planning and advisory (7%)
- Capital raising (4%)

Out of these, payments is the largest segment with 68 entities working and providing services in South Africa. There can be seen as an alignment with international trends, where the payment segment is the major portion of the FinTech landscape. So, overall FinTech adoption in South Africa stands at 82%.

2.10 CHINA

The largest FinTech market worldwide, China has been leading other nations in FinTech growth. FinTech agreements in China totaled $25.5 billion in 2018, nine times higher than the previous year. According to estimates, 46% of all FinTech investments made worldwide in 2018 were in China. The consumer adoption rate contributes 87% as well. China's being at the forefront of FinTech is not something unexpected. FinTech enables it to bounce over conventional banking systems significant to developed nations because the Chinese financial system was not well-developed. This leads to opening up an opportunity for tech establishments such as Alibaba and Tencent to grab the space and provide FinTech based financial services.

Nowadays, mobile phones are used for most transactions in China. Additionally, China's regulatory frameworks are less restrictive than those in the West, which also attempts to strengthen the infrastructure for FinTech, when it comes to accepting it. Chinese FinTechs are primarily concentrated in the domestic payments market, particularly in retail. The majority of Chinese banks have given technology companies this market share. These technology companies created new ecosystem models (FinTech) extremely quickly to serve customers through super-apps for smartphones.

Thus, it delivers a remarkable customer experience in terms of usability, simplicity, and convenience. The blend of favorable market conditions and regulatory environment has thrived Chinese FinTech to global leadership.

2.11 INDIA

Due to the acceleration of business growth and employment creation, FinTech is currently one of the most flourishing industries. The global FinTech software and services market, according to NASSCOM, is projected to reach $45 billion by 2020, growing at a 7.1% CAGR (BFSI Post, 2020). India has risen to become the second-largest FinTech hub in the world and is currently going through a "FinTech Boom." With almost $270 million in investments in 2016, India is among the top five markets for equity financing and investments thanks to the over 2000 FinTechs that operate in this manner. FinTech in India is still in its infancy, but it is quickly becoming a necessary component of daily operations. From a larger viewpoint, it is crucially promoting financial inclusion in the nation.

The move of transforming traditional services into a digital platform has proved worthwhile for customers as well as businesses, including independent workers, rural entrepreneurs, small lenders and borrowers, and small and medium industries. India is a country with the world's second biggest population who are not even aware of banking services. Here FinTech has to play a significant role in the financial inclusion of the unbanked population thus breaking barriers such as the following:

- Lack of financial literacy
- Huge cost associated with traditional banking services
- Lack of efficiency and transparency
- Lack of decision making

2.12 SCOPE OF FINTECH

FinTech's reach lies in expanding the market, understanding customer behavior, and influencing long-term changes in the financial sector. The role of financial technologies in the financial inclusion is huge if the key factors are considered by startups such as relevant experience in the financial services industry, Customer-centric business models, and strategic partnerships between the financial institutions and FinTech (Soriano, 2017). FinTech startups are likely to lower prices and provide high-level financial services. FinTech companies will expand unique and progressive problem assessment systems. Leveraging big data, providing experience on how to subscribe to credit scores, and increasing credit ratings for customers with limited credit records will improve the penetration of financial services in India.

FinTech will create a diversified, secure, and solid landscape for financial services. FinTech factories are less homogeneous than consolidated banks and provide world-class solutions for skills improvement and a regular working environment. FinTech is anticipated to broaden the short-term insurance solutions that are popular worldwide and now entering partnerships to serve customer demands from all backgrounds. This approach is expected to be more helpful by following a more proactive and tactical mechanism toward insecure interfaces. Deploying a combination of multi-layer encryption, behavioral biometrics, and controlling the frauds in real-time are some instruments to control cyber vulnerabilities and minimize risks that will emerge with the increasing exposure of FinTech applications.

Most of the financial institutions have partnered with FinTech organizations at different levels; public and private will be on the rise, and other mutual synergies will also lead to maintaining favorable situations in the FinTech industry.

2.13 CHALLENGES OF FINTECH

FinTech, an emerging technology offers a wide range of opportunities but also poses various roadblocks for organizations and various stakeholders (Kundariya, 2019).

2.14 CYBERCRIME IN FINANCE

The primary responsibility of financial institutions is to keep the data of customers 100% safe but as there are technological innovations, it is hard to keep the data protected from cybercrimes. So many measures have been taken by various FinTech organizations and this issue is addressed by Distributed ledger technology (blockchain). As more FinTech industries are emerging, the blockchain industry plays a crucial role to control this issue.

2.15 BIG DATA USE IN FINANCE

The Big Data platform provides FinTech service providers with opportunities and challenges. The banks will now better serve their customers via social networking, consumer services, and various news sources. But there's very little torrent for organizing unstructured data into useful information. Innovative technology for data processing is therefore required to take advantage of this. Also, data analytics solutions with manageable operations, risks, and more financial services are on the rise more than ever before.

2.16 FINTECH DISRUPTION OF FINANCIAL INDUSTRY

The evolution of small FinTech organizations that emerged less than a decade ago was unable to show the potential growth that was expected at the time of their birth. On the contrary, most other companies can turn into large companies. This is due to the asymmetrical distribution of FinTech technologies. Therefore, estimating the growth potential of any organization has become difficult. Understanding the current scenario, applying FinTech technology safely is a difficult situation.

2.17 CROSSING THE DIGITAL DIVIDE IN FINANCIAL SERVICES

The digital banking platform is not just about installing a mobile application; It is more than that. Their goal is to digitize the whole brand, which is not an easy task. For example, if an organization adopts some traditional advertising media advertising campaigns on a digital network, it is possible to do so in this technological era. With this, companies will be able to reach their target audience in this competitive environment. This type of presence in social media is necessary, and Facebook ads and google ads will make this work much easier. It will also allow us to tap into big data, Artificial Intelligence to find potential customers and to provide them with customized services in a minimum of time. Developing a brand using social media platforms is critical and therefore businesses should look into such issues as early as possible.

2.18 CUSTOMER EXPERIENCE IN THE FINANCIAL SERVICE

One of the main challenges facing most FinTech companies in the financial services industry is the best customer experience. Today, banking customers have the priority of getting mobile banking, and they are less aware of the compatibility of banking services with or not FinTech. Carrying conventional banking systems to an online platform is a time-consuming process. However, most of the FinTech and banks are collaborating these days to enhance financial services.

2.19 REGULATORY COMPLIANCE IN FINANCE

Before the adoption of any innovation or technology, it is foremost to comply with government rules and regulations. Thus, it is observed that the regulatory environment is unstable; the financial organizations have to face persistent challenges. RegTech, being an emerging technology, can help overcome the compliance problem. By applying FinTech's cutting-edge technologies to report regulatory compliance, RegTech startups can successfully bridge the gap between the financial services industry and its regulations. It can be useful for optimizing automated processes and reporting and auditing.

2.20 CUSTOMER RETENTION IN FINANCIAL SERVICES

Customer retention is the primary motivation of any company or sector to stay long term. The FinTech organization can provide personalized, excellent, automated services, and better access, which is the most important thing for customers. The benefits of effectively serving the customer base will lead to a greater market share. So, the first step to not losing market share is to get to know your customers, their demand, and their concerns. Serving customers with what they want is the reason for the business.

2.21 EMPLOYEE RETENTION IN THE FINANCIAL INDUSTRY

In the financial service industry, acquiring human resources with the right skills and abilities is as difficult as attracting customers, and if companies find such an employee, short-term employment is another big issue. Good pay and incentives are not enough to retain employees; now I am looking for a better nature, working conditions, and lifestyle for the employer. To survive in this competitive world, constant changes are necessary to overcome the most important challenges one must think more than just victories; companies must use natural benefits efficiently; lead to growth and work intelligently.

There are many other challenges that FinTech Application has to face:

- Small management teams
- Less availability of credit and startup experience
- Limited financial resources
- Unknown target market or business model
- Nascent data analysis technologies
- Burden from the investors to swiftly establish the operations
- Limited knowledge about financial compliances

2.22 CONCLUSION

FinTech adoption is driven by a wide range of demand-side and supply-side factors. It is observed that FinTech will lead to financial inclusion and will bring most of the population to the digital platform. The high cost associated with traditional banking and finance will surface if there will be more collaborations between financial institutions and FinTechs. Thus, it shows the importance of regulatory factors that play a crucial role but regulatory frameworks do not seem to be a primary driver of FinTech adoption to date.

Population aging and constant evolution in technologies and FinTech may have a major impact on the future direction of the FinTech adoption rate. FinTech global adoption may also enhance the financial inter-linkages across the cross-borders. Yet FinTech services still require adequate regulation and supervision. There is evidence that there is a plethora of FinTech companies emerging worldwide with a range of financial services.

The global adoption rate of financial technologies is ever-growing. Many firms try to grow and innovate through in-house technological innovations, but most of the firms outsource through incubators, accelerators, etc. Transforming the traditional banking system into a cashless digital platform is a challenge in terms of the level of adoption by the population worldwide. FinTech organizations despite having huge opportunities have still gone through a long path.

KEYWORDS

- financial technology
- gross domestic product
- fintech evolution
- technology acceptance model
- RegTech

REFERENCES

Accenture. The Future of Fintech and Banking: Digitally Disrupted or Reimagined? 2015.

Adinarayana, P. J.; KishoreBabu, B. Modern Techniques of Promoting the Banking Financial Services and Insurance (Bsfi). *Regular Issue* **2019,** *8* (10), 1715–1719. https://doi.org/10.35940/ijitee.j9044.0881019

Agarwal, S.; Hauswald, R. Distance and Private Information in Lending. *Rev. Financial Stud.* **2010,** *23* (7), 2757–2788. https://doi.org/10.1093/rfs/hhq001

Alexander, S. *What Drives Fintech Adoption in Countries,* Feb 13, 2020. https://www.livemint.com/industry/banking/what-drives-fintech-adoption-in-countries-11581614845081.html

AL Shaer, D. S.; Hamdan, A.; Razzaque, A. Social Media Enhances Consumer Behaviour During E-Transactions: An Empirical Evidence from Bahrain. *J. Inform. Knowledge Manage.* **2020,** *19* (01), 2040012. https://doi.org/10.1142/s0219649220400122

Bhandari, M. India and the Pyramid of Opportunity. *The FinTech Book* **2016,** 81–83. https://doi.org/10.1002/9781119218906.ch22

Boons, F.; Lüdeke-Freund, F. Business Models for Sustainable Innovation: State-of-the-Art and Steps Towards a Research Agenda. *J. Clean. Product* **2013,** *45*, 9–19.

Chesbrough, H. W. Business Model Innovation: It's Not Just About Technology Anymore. *Strategy Leadership* **2007,** *35* (6), 12–17.

Desai, F. *The Evolution of Fintech. Forbes*, Feb 9, 2016. https://www.forbes.com/sites/falgunidesai/2015/12/13/the-evolution-of-fintech/#615a32997175

DeYoung, R.; Glennon, D.; Nigro, P. J. Borrower-Lender Distance, Credit Scoring, and the Performance of Small Business Loans, 2006.

Douglas, J. L. New Wine Into Old Bottles: Fintech Meets the Bank Regulatory World. *North Carolina Bank. Inst.* **2016,** *20* (1), 17.

FintechAdoptioninNorthAmericaLagsGlobalAcceptance.TheFinancialBrand,Jan30,2020. https://thefinancialbrand.com/92575/banking-fintech-adoption-north-america-trends/

Fintech in China: What Lies Ahead. Wharton University of Pennsylvania, 2019. https://knowledge.wharton.upenn.edu/article/fintech-china-lies-ahead/

FinTech in India: A Revolution Is Underway. BFSI Post, 2020. https://bfsi.eletsonline.com/fintech-in-india-a-revolution-is-underway/#:~:text=FinTech%20is%20amongst%20the%20most,%25%2C%20reveals%20data%20from%20NASSCOM

Fintech in the USA. Lexology, Jan 24, 2019. https://www.lexology.com/library/detail.aspx?g=3e179d35-3b0b-4725-b511-1ee5c8e56701

Fintech Login Gets an India, China Lift. The Economic Times, Aug. 23, 2019. https://economictimes.Indiatimes.com/industry/banking/Finance/Fintech-login-gets-an-India-the china-liFt/articleshow/70796850.cms?From=mdr

Ghosh, I. *Visualizing the Current Landscape of the Fintech Industry,* Jan. 28, 2020. https://markets.businessinsider.com/news/stocks/current-fintech-industry-1028852418

Global FinTech Adoption Index. EY FinTech Australia Census 2019, 2019. https://fintechauscensus.ey.com/2019/Documents/ey-global-fintech-adoption-index-2019.pdf

Haddad, C.; Hornuf, L. The Emergence of the Global Fintech Market: Economic and Technological Determinants. *SSRN Electronic Journal, 2016*. https://doi.org/10.2139/ssrn.2830124

Hu, Z., Ding, S., Li, S., Chen, L., & Yang, S. Adoption Intention of Fintech Services for Bank Users: An Empirical Examination with an Extended Technology Acceptance Model. *Symmetry* **2019,** *11* (3), 340. https://doi.org/10.3390/sym11030340

Kundariya, H. *The Challenges of Fintech Application in Modern Era—A Comprehensive Guide*. Customer Think, Dec 9, 2019. https://customerthink.com/the-challenges-of-fintech-application-in-modern-era-a-comprehensive-guide/

Leong, K.; Sung, A. FinTech (Financial Technology): What Is It and How to Use Technologies to Create Business Value in Fintech Way? *Int. J. Innov. Manage. Technol. 2018*, 74–78. https://doi.org/10.18178/ijimt.2018.9.2.791

Parameshwar, H. S.; Sruthie, A.; Cisse, M.; Kumar, M. A.; Misra, S. Fintech and Disruptions: An Impact Assessment. *J. Crit. Rev.* **2019,** *6* (6), 89–97.

Pierri, N.; Timmer, Y. Tech in Fin before FinTech. *IMF Working Papers* **2020,** *20* (14). https://doi.org/10.5089/9781513519258.001

Priya, P. K.; Anusha, K. Fintech Issues and Challenges in India. *Int. J. Recent Technol. Eng.* **2019,** *8* (3), 904–908. https://doi.org/10.35940/ijrte.c4087.098319

Saksonova, S.; Kuzmina-Merlino, I. Fintech as Financial Innovation—The Possibilities and Problems of Implementation. *Eur. Res. Stud. J.* **2017,** *XX* (3A), 961–973. https://doi.org/10.35808/ersj/757

Shaping the Future of Financial Services. The Global City, 2020. https://www.theglobalcity.uk/fintech

Soriano, M. A. Factors Driving Financial Inclusion and Financial Performance in Fintech New Ventures: An Empirical Study. Dissertations and Theses Collection (Open Access) 2017, 1–258. https://ink.library.smu.edu.sg/etd_coll/145

The Global Expansion of FinTech. Translate Media, Nov 9, 2018. https://www.translatemedia.com/translation-blog/the-global-expansion-of-fintech/

CHAPTER 3

Fintech Disruptions in Financial Sector: Opportunities, Challenges, and Future

NEHA PURI[1] and HARJIT SINGH[2, 3]

[1] *Amity University, Noida Campus, Uttar Pradesh, India*

[2] *Symbiosis Centre for Management Studies Noida, India*

[3] *Symbiosis International University Pune, India*

ABSTRACT

Fintech is bringing change in economies across the globe. Fintech comprises a wide variety of products, innovations, and business models which are changing the financial services market. Financial can be described as a next platform for growth that explains the intersection between technology and financial services. It involves everything from cashless transfers to crowdfunding sites, robo advisors, and virtual currencies. Financial firms have used technology to improve services for a long period of time. Financial technology is a new technology and innovation which seeks to compete with conventional financial methods and financial service delivery. Using smart phones for mobile banking, investment services, and cryptocurrency are examples of technology that seeks to make technology more accessible to users. Financial technology companies can establish start-up to provide the services to the every person at their doorstep. Fintech is a new financial sector that is using technology to improve its financial activities.

Revolutionary Challenges and Opportunities of Fintech. Shweta Anand, PhD, Shalini Srivastav, PhD, Vikas Garg, PhD, & Geetika Garg (Eds.)

3.1 INTRODUCTION

The financial technology sector comprises technology-enabled companies offering financial services, as well as supplying software services to financial institutions, directly. Fintech firms use technologies to facilitate enterprise and customer financial transactions. Technological developments, rising competition for financial goods, and financial services innovation are all behind a new generation of Fintech start-ups and acquisitions that have drawn industry interest in recent years. Digital Finance includes a variety of new financial goods, financial ventures, finance-related applications, and new ways of customer contact and interaction—provided by Fintech firms and creative financial service providers (Gomber, 2017). E-finance is defined as "the method or process of financial services and markets using electronic communication and computation." Three E-finance fields were focused on the use of electronic payment systems, the development of financial services firms, and the use of financial machinery (Allen, 2002). Seven gaps were identified, such as change required in industrial and organization structure of financial services, availability of alternative finance like loan-based crowdfunding, changes in the mechanism of payments in order to move toward a cashless society, reaching customers in remote areas, Calculation, artificial intelligence, and large-scale financial data processing; the relationship between emerging financial technology and financial regulation and identity, surveillance, data protection, and financial services regulation (Milne, 2018). According to Spiros Margaris (Fintech expert), "The Fintech Industry has the potential to have its biggest positive impact on the lives of the unbanked of this world. And that's, In my eyes, The Magic in The Making." Fintech is anything that uses technology in the financial sector. The key Fintech areas are:

1. Business Process Outsourcing
2. Investments and capital market tech
3. Digital Lending
4. E-Commerce and Marketing Tech
5. Financial Media and Data Solution
6. Insurance and Healthcare tech
7. Payments
8. HR and Payroll Tech
9. Security Technology

FIGURE 3.1 Various areas of Fintech technology.

Fintech technology is related to money transfer or transactions and that goes like payments to bank and how money is manage/transferred. Fintech describes any business that uses internet, conventional devices, software technology, or cloud services to connect with financial services. Fintech firms' technologies are transforming the ways many people handle and making their investments simpler. It provides ample options to participate in financial services, such as crowdfunding, block chain, mobile payments, insurtech, stock-trading apps. Fintech has developed business to business, business to client options in the financial sector.

3.2 OVERVIEW OF THE INDIAN FINTECH MARKET

FinTech is ranked among the most successful industries in terms of both business growth and economic development. India emerges as a third largest Fintech technology. According to Accenture, "Fintech investments in the country nearly doubled to $3.7 billion in 2019, up from $1.9 billion the previous year, which puts it a third spot after the US and UK." The transition from conventional to digital payments has proved beneficial for both individuals and companies, including self-employed, rural businessmen, small lenders, and small- and medium-sized enterprises. In a nation with the second largest unbanked population in the world, FinTech played a crucial role in breaking down obstacles, such as lack of financial literacy, high cost of conventional banking services, and policy differences that restrict a significant percentage of Indians from becoming part of the formal financial landscape. India has continued to witness the FinTech evolutionary upsurge, which is primarily compounded by the emergence of new FinTech start-ups and a robust wave of technological advances. India FinTech industry has shown a tremendous growth over a period of 5 years. From January 2013 to October 2013, roughly 2000 FinTech firms were established in 2018, turning India into a hotbed for entrepreneurship. Rachit Chawla, founder and CEO of Finway, says that the economy needs a concerted effort from all branches of government to accelerate growth, particularly after we experienced a slowdown in growth last year as a result of numerous internal and external factors like the IL&FS crisis and the China–US trade war. I'm pleased with what this budget can accomplish for all of us if it is completely implemented. The Indian Fintech sector has grown significantly during the last few years. Paytm, Pine Labs, PayU, and Faircent are a few of the well-known Fintech start-ups that are slowly making India their home base. The foundation of the Fintech ecosystem is the idea of collaboration and integration with other organizations, where the opportunities play a key role. Below are the main stakeholders mentioned in Figure 3.1, which identify this industry's success.

3.2.1 START-UPS

India currently boasts over 600 Fintech start-ups belonging to different sectors, and it is predicted that the number will grow, particularly with the launch of initiatives such as a based accelerator system by local and state governments and banks. In fact, the strategic assistance is provided by major companies and venture capital. A makeover is actually under way for the start-ups.

3.2.2 EDUCATIONAL INSTITUTIONS

Academic institutions play a significant part in influencing the potential entrepreneurs' mind set. Recently, leading organizations in India have been playing a constructive role in coordinating activities and competitions as well as in delivering professional instruction. For example, the Global Entrepreneur Conclave was arranged by IIT Roorkee, one of our country's leading institutions.

3.2.3 GOVERNMENT AND REGULATORS

Government and regulation authority plays an important role in supporting Fintech companies financially. Various schemes have been launched by government such as Start-Up Initiatives. The regulatory authorities, such as SEBI and RBI are also encouraging Fintech companies in achieving the country's dream of being a cashless economy.

3.2.4 FINANCIAL INSTITUTIONS

With the accelerated growth of the Fintech market, various BFSIs partner with Fintech start-ups on a range of sites, such as wallets and online customer acquisition, among others. They provide creative start-ups with constructive mentorship, encouragement, and funding. For example, Bank of India offers a wallet driven by TechProcess, in partnership with Paynimo.

3.2.5 INCUBATORS AND ACCELERATORS

Incubators and accelerators have a role not only in finance, but also in developing the financial system and enhancing soft skills. Financial institutions play a major role in talent discovery and the development of platforms and remedies.

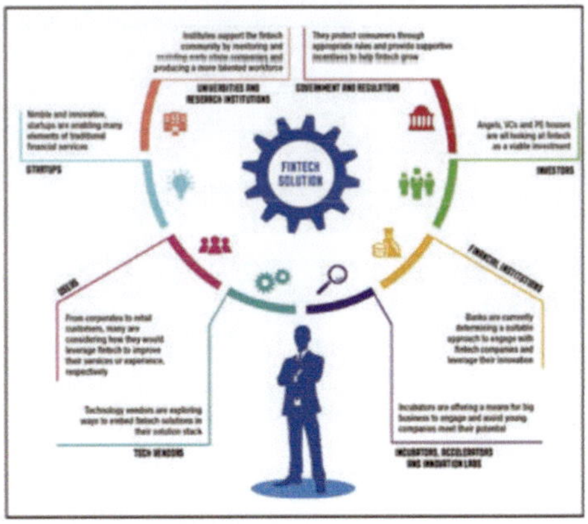

FIGURE 3.2 Pillars of a Fintech ecosystem.
Source: https://www.forbesindia.com/article/special/fintech-firms-more-enablers-than-disruptors-kpmgnasscom-report/43455/1

3.2.6 USERS

Users, consisting of both individuals and organizations in the form of consumers, have shown remarkable acceptability to the technology-driven transition of India's economy. Daily cash transactions have given way to cashless and mobile banking transactions.

3.3 KEY DRIVERS OF INDIAN FINTECH REVOLUTION

The industry in the financial services sector is marked by new technologies and business models that are driven by technology. Its development was primarily a function in the respective markets of the inherent excesses, inefficiencies, and unexplored opportunities. Indian Fintech's main drives were explained in the diagram given below: -

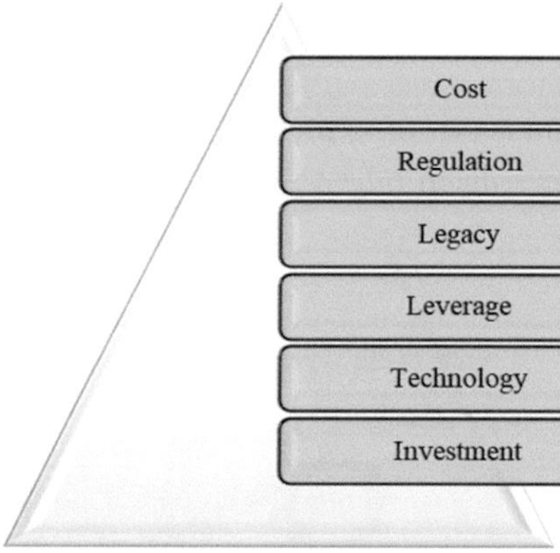

FIGURE 3.3 Fintech's key drivers.
Source: Authors' compilation.

3.3.1 COST

Cost is an effective tool in the Fintech industry. In more than 100 years, since the global financial crisis, the rate of financial intermediation remained largely constant. Fintech's advances have largely been about reducing this cost, moving from cash to cashless economy.

3.3.2 REGULATION

Indian regulation governs the different forms of financial services. Indian securities consulting research includes a license as an investment adviser. Fintech goods and services can be found by and wide to come under the purview of regulators, such as RBI, SEBI, MEITY, and IRDAI.

3.3.3 LEGACY

The world has been changed by revolutionary emerging technology, such as artificial intelligence (AI), machine learning, and the Internet of Things (IoT). Customers are increasingly seeking customized services, and firms who have not digitized their industries need to change to succeed in this modern environment. Many banks are still saddled with stiff, core legacy applications.

3.3.4 LEVERAGE

Taking advantage of the FinTech possibilities in India and bringing forward useful ideas in the form of informative writing-ups provided by both existing and emerging FinTech industry players. Although the FinTech industry offers creativity and innovative technology, banks will boost demand from the customers. It is up to banks to harness and incorporate these principles and innovative ideas into their own style. In coming days, banks are expected to absorb and incorporate FinTech innovations into their usual course of operation.

3.3.5 TECHNOLOGY

Usage of mobile phones is important for acceptance and development in FinTech services, particularly in those countries, where there is limited access to Orthodox Banking. GSMA evidence suggests that for single, global mobile subscriptions today, penetration is 65% and is expected to hit through 2020, 73%. Around the same time, the use of smartphones grows from 51 to 65%.

3.3.6 INVESTMENT

Crowdfunding sites have done something similar and have been a significant funding vehicle for many seed-stage companies. Such sites link individuals looking to make small investments in start-ups with a range of possible investment goals and encourage the "wisdom of the crowd" to determine whether the businesses will be funded and will not be funded (with a slice of funds being taken by those that are funded successfully).

3.4 SEGMENT OVERVIEW: AREAS, PRODUCTS, AND SERVICES (DIGITAL PAYMENTS)

Digital payment systems are quickly replacing the existing payment forms that required physical interaction between buyers and sellers with the innovation of telecommunication. Digital payment mechanisms include electronic financial transfers using some digital financial instrument forms, such as e-tokens, e-cash, and checks. Digital payment systems offer a number of benefits to the individuals and business organizations. Indian Government has taken many initiatives to market and initiate online transactions in the country. One of the initiative, "Digital India" Campaign was started by government which aimed at creating digitally empowered economy. To understand it simply, a digital payment happens when products or services are bought using different electronic media. This form of payment system does not use cash or cheques. The primary aim of digital transactions is to reduce the costs and risks of handling cash and to make transactions easier to conduct. According to Razorpay's report on "The Era of Rising Fintech" shows digital transactions grew by 338% from 2018 to 2019 with UPI and card transactions seeing the highest growth. Figure 3.4 demonstrates the different categories of digital payments: -

3.4.1 BANKING CARDS

Banking cards give customers greater protection, comfort, and power than any other form of payment. The wide variety of available cards—including credit, debit, and prepaid cards—also provides enormous flexibility. To secure purchases, these cards have two-factor authentication, for example, secure PIN and OTP. Several examples of card payment schemes include RuPay, Paypal, MasterCard.

Digital Payments	Banking Cards USSD Aadhaar Enabled Payment System (AEPS) UPI
	Mobile Wallets Bank pre-paid cards Point of Sale (PoS)
	Internet Banking Mobile Banking Bharat Interface for Money (BHIM) app

FIGURE 3.4 Categories of digital payments.
Source: Authors' Compilation.

3.4.2 USSD (UNSTRUCTURED SUPPLEMENTARY SERVICE DATA)

This service enables mobile banking transfers using basic cell phone function, there is no need to have mobile internet access facility to use mobile banking based on USSD. This is meant to include financial deepening and the inclusion in the traditional banking system of underbanked society.

3.4.3 AADHAAR-ENABLED PAYMENT SYSTEM (AEPS)

It can be utilized for all banking operations, including transfers from Aadhaar to Aadhaar funds, cash withdrawals, cash deposits, and loan inquiries. Every transfer is routed through a banking correspondent using Aadhaar authentication. There's no need to visit a branch personally, have debit or credit cards or even sign a contract. The customer can avail this service, if his/her Aadhaar number is registered with bank in which the account is being operated.

3.4.4 UPI

UPI is a form of interoperable payment network through which any client keeping a bank account can send and receive money through a UPI-based application. The service helps a customer to connect more than one bank account to their mobile on a UPI device to easily facilitate fund transactions and accept requests 24/7 for all 365 days a year.

3.4.5 MOBILE WALLETS

Mobile wallets in India are expanding rapidly. According to a report by BI Mobile Payments, electronic payments in-store will be rising to $503 billion by 2020. Mobile transaction size will rise 10-fold by 2021 according to another survey. Cash or credit card can be conveniently placed on mobile wallets. Some of the examples of mobile wallet apps in the market are Paytm, Mobikwik, Freecharge, etc.

3.4.6 BANK PRE-PAID CARDS

A prepaid card is a form of payment instrument that can load money to make transactions. Bank pre-paid card is not connected to customer's bank account. A debit card issued by the bank is therefore connected to the customer's checking account.

3.4.7 POINT OF SALE (POS)

PoS terminals historically referred to those that were mounted at all retailers where consumers make payments using credit/debit cards. Typically, it is a hand-held device that reads bank cards.

3.4.8 INTERNET BANKING

A system that enables customers to do both financial and non-financial activities from their net banking accounts is referred to as this. The user can transfer money from his account into other accounts at the same bank or another bank using a website or electronic program.

3.4.9 MOBILE BANKING

Mobile banking is a service provided by a bank or other financial institution that enables its customers to carry out various types of financial transactions directly using a mobile device, like a cell phone or laptop. It makes use of programs, often known as apps, that are supported for that reason by banks or other financial institutions.

3.4.10 BHARAT INTERFACE FOR MONEY (BHIM) APP

Bharat Interface for Money (BHIM) is a payment system that uses the Unified Payments Interface (UPI) to render quick, convenient, and fast transactions. Using their UPI ID, or scanning the QR with the BHIM app, you can make direct bank transfers to someone on UPI.

3.5 KEY EMERGING TRENDS

There is a long list of factors at play that will shape the future projection of the Indian Fintech Market. Here, we intend to look at the following prominent key trends that are crucial to driving this growth.

3.5.1 ARTIFICIAL INTELLIGENCE (AI)

In the last one decade, artificial intelligence or machine learning has made many remarkable advancements across multiple industries. Retail is not an exception. Though not every retailer has been using artificial intelligence due to expensive technology but the big players, such as Amazon, Walmart, Carrefour, Costco, Tesco, Flipkart, and Dominos have been very active about this. For instance, retail artificial intelligence is capable enough to study human behavior, learn their preferences, tastes, likings, and disliking. The modern applications of AI are so capable that they can know what the customer wants, when they want, and in which way they prefer goods and services. Consequently, AI applications can reveal a number of ways to provide personal experience to the customers, resulting in enhanced customer experience, selection, speed, and quality.

3.5.2 HYPERLOCAL

Hyperlocal, as per literary mean, refers to a localized area, such as a nearby society, a small town, or even a metro city, such as Delhi and Mumbai. The two basic principles on which the concept of hyperlocal works on are geography and time. Hyperlocal retailers are described start-ups that supply things from confined stores to ultimate consumers through an armada of delivery agents.

In addition to supplying goods and services listed by provisional stores and shoppers, hyperlocal applications also allow customers to place general orders which can be contented from any or many stores and that is only in 24–48 h depending upon the size of the local area. For instance, Amazon has first announced its Prime service, which assured 48 hours or simply saying two-day delivery at customer's doorstep, it earned an enormous appreciation among consumers worldwide.

Hyperlocal services may be offered by new start-ups such as Swiggy and Zomoto that as such do not hold any retail outlet of their own or it may be offered by the established retailers with the same speed and door delivery, such as Flipkart, Amazon, and so on. To stay ahead in competition and meet rising consumers' demand, Amazon, Dominos, and many more retailers have been experimenting with drone delivery. Thanks to Hyperlocal, local offline, and unorganized retailers which were on the verge of dying, got a new lease of life for their business.

3.5.3 ULTRA OR HYPER PERSONALIZATION

The time of offering aggregate experiences is now coming to an end. Shoppers cannot just subdivide their customers into single bucket and generate common marketing promotions. Mass promotional techniques are becoming outdated. Therefore, a new era of "customized experiences" was introduced in metro/big cities, such as Delhi, Bangalore, and Mumbai. But with modern buyers gradually trusting on mobile apps, extremely tailored shop experiences are turning inevitable. Technical advancements that help consumers make a buying decision quicker are essential. Nowadays, ultra-personalization has been becoming one of the most indispensable constituents of driving enhanced adaptations.

Particularly in verticals such as Banks, Insurance, and Electronics, clients have come to trust on e-commerce web portals to indorse their succeeding buying. Purchase likings are analyzed along several viewpoints by learning the method they relate with the online gateway, analyzing their assessments, and reflecting the buying behaviors to ultimately offer personalized product endorsements, campaigns, and commercials. The faster the sellers jump on this movement, the improved are their probabilities of remembering clients and gaining market segment.

3.5.4 VOICE SEARCH

Voice-activated systems, such as Alexa, Siri, OK Google, and Cortana are gradually ingratiating themselves into our daily lives. We require assistance frequently in our daily lives. For instance, voice search is essential when you are cooking and need to verify a recipe but your hands are covered in flour. It is a well-liked hands-free technique for getting traffic updates or information about nearby businesses while driving. For a trader's success, voice search app optimization is therefore becoming increasingly important. The following are typical advantages of optimizing for voice searches: They can more easily multitask thanks to technology, and it also gives them the power to access information and solutions right away, as well as to solve problems more quickly than they could using traditional methods.

3.5.5 INNOVATIVE AND SOCIAL SHOPPING

Retailers have been using innovative stories and experiences to attract customers. By using AI-powered 360-degree videos, customers are provided feel and satisfaction of goods and services before buying. For instance, a 360-degree view, copy, or audio-visual of a model tiring a dress is displayed online then offline. Where video provides feel, comfort, trend, and look, audio narrates stories and provide feedback.

Video plus rich media text offer novel and fascinating methods for buyers to discern new goods and involve with the e-commerce podium. Once suitable, one can also use animated GIFs to better display case products, its usefulness and its advantages. Besides innovative content, social media is being widely used as an emerging marketing and communication tool, a discussion board for novel thoughts, a source of info on shopper taste buds, along with selling windows.

3.5.6 CHECKOUT-FREE STORES

Self-checkout stores or commonly called self-service checkout are semi-attended customer-activated terminal (SACAT) machineries that offer a platform for shoppers to route their own buying from a trader. They offer a substitute to the old-fashioned cashier handled checkout. The client does the task of the teller themselves, by scanning and applying imbursement for the items. For example, Amazon Go's cashier less outlets, which practice cameras and instrument learning and intricate sensors to permit clients to just pick up what they require and come out have become fashion of the day.

In Self-checkout stores, prior to enter a store, a shopper has to image his store-specific App like in the case of Amazon, it is "Amazon Go app" that embraces their credit card details. Once they enter the outlet, they are traced and sensored, and in case if they pick something from the shelf, then that particular item gets added to his/her virtual cart, and in case they keep it back on the shelf, things taken are out of his/her computer-generated cart. Once the selection is complete and customer passes through the gated barrier with the item, he/she is billed for those items.

Though in some part of the world, several problems have been informed with this system specifically the inexactness of body-scanning and the incapability to keep record of items moved by kids, this progressive technology has paved the way for a more well-organized shopping age, where lengthy point of sale queues are now outdated. Imagine checkout-free outlets to become the common rule in the near future.

3.6 CHALLENGES FACED BY FINTECH ECOSYSTEM

Undoubtedly, Fintech has been playing vital character in getting automation in business processes. With the advantage of emerging know-hows, institutions especially the financial such as banks are able to save billions of dollars annually. But there are several roadblocks in the development and growth of Fintech. The prominent among them are as follows:

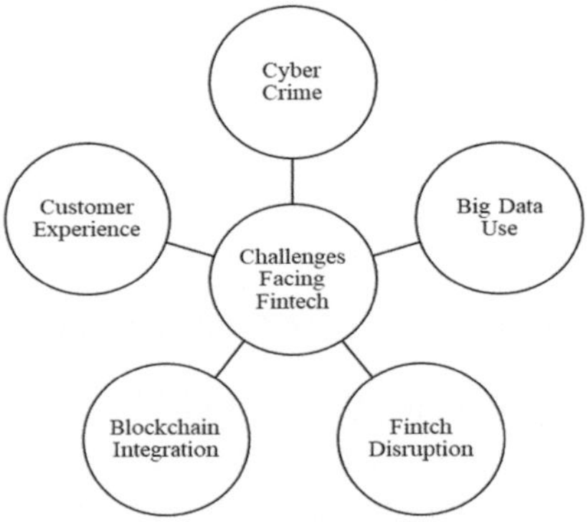

FIGURE 3.5 Challenges faced by Fintech ecosystem.
Source: Compiled by authors.

3.6.1 CYBERCRIME

Although the financial institutions have been trying their level best to protect the customer data, it becomes difficult for them also. There are several cybercrime answers that Fintech businesses offer; nonetheless, the Blockchain technology is the prominent one to regulate such issue. The reason is that the way new businesses are developing everyday, the financial commerce has to gaze for the best possible answers.

3.6.2 BIG DATA USAGE IN FINANCE DOMAIN

The Big Database science compromises both prospects and challenges before Fintech technology benefactors. With the advent of social media and customer databases, banks, insurers, and share brokers can aid their clients in an improved way. But flow for cataloguing the formless data for beneficial data is very trivial. Hence, it necessities an influential data analytics know-how to manage business operations, risks, and monetary services.

3.6.3 FINTECH DISRUPTION IN FINANCIAL TRADE

The Fintech concerns, especially emerged in last one decade, find it difficult to display the probable development, which was expected at the period of their appearance. While some further are capable to grow into a large firm. The intention may be due to the uneven circulation of Fintech technologies, making it difficult to calculate the growth potential for any company. In this situation, Creating Fintech Application benign and safe is a big challenge.

3.7 THE BLOCKCHAIN INTEGRATION IN FINANCE INDUSTRY

As discussed earlier, blockchain has gradually emerged as a key technology in battling against the cybercrime. But when it comes to financial sector, "privacy of data" is not the only application of the blockchain. Blockchain plays a vital role in the delivery and transaction of financial instruments. However, experts opine that industry-wide implementation of the blockchain is fairly challenging.

3.8 CUSTOMER EXPERIENCE

Internet banking or better say online banking is not fair about using a mobile application. It is considerable beyond that. It emphasizes on digitizing the entire brand. Any company that implements digitization in their operational dealings, tracks the improved advertising campaigns from traditional ad-media to online channels, they are capable to compete domestically and internationally. Social media explosion, such as Google ads, Facebook, and usage of artificial intelligence (AI) make work easy and faster. Therefore, it is inevitable that companies should take care of these technological developments and plan accordingly.

3.9 FUTURE OF FINTECH

The rate at which disruption has been occurring in the financial services industry, presents huge opportunities for Fintech technology to prosper. Though initially Fintech technology was widely used as the back-office support function for bankers and insurers. Start-ups, venture capitalists, and public sector enterprises (PSEs) hardly invested in the Fintech technology. But, industry reports depict that from 2019 onwards, and things have changes drastically. Private venture capital increased rapidly and the share of investment across globe increased from 5% to nearly 25%—a level equal to the fair share of GDP indorsed to the financial industry. In short, Fintech has found its space in the innovation economy. The Fintech adoption rate across globe has been presented in Figure 3.6.

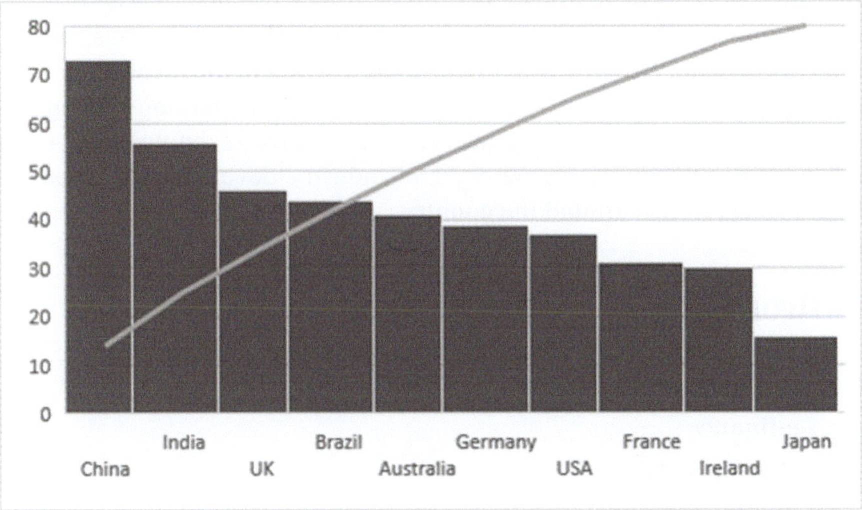

FIGURE 3.6 Fintech adoption rate across globe.
Source: Compiled by authors.

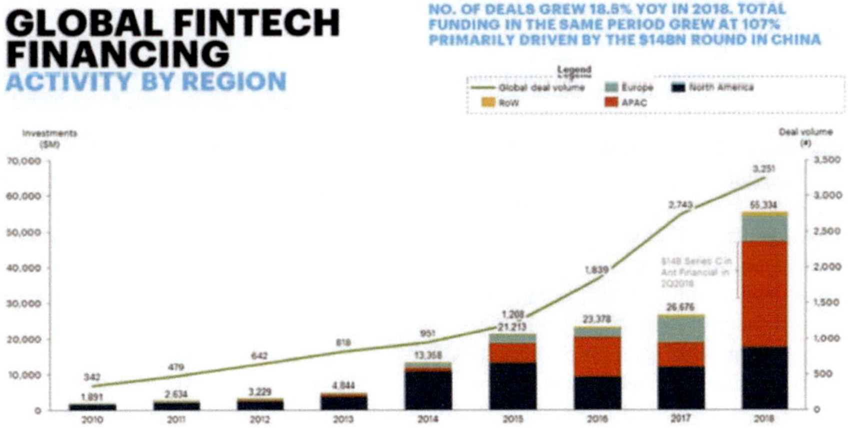

FIGURE 3.7 Global Fintech financing.
Source: https://newsroom.accenture.com/news/global-fintech-investments-surged-in-2018-with-investments-in-china-taking-the-lead-accenture-analysis-finds-uk-gains-sharply-despite-brexit-doubts.htm

The increasing Fintech adoption rate will directly have its impact on banks, private equity, insurers, hedge funds, consulting firms, venture capitalist, auditing firms, and so on. Experts do not find any reason that Fintech will reduce the impact that these firms have, and instead of being restraining for these firms, it will absolutely disrupt the business by improving them. Besides this, Fintech has also led to the creation of some dynamic industries, such as WealthTech (Wealth Technology), RegTech (Regulatory Technology), and InsurTech (Insurance Technology). In short, all industry indicators, regulatory and industry developments present a bright future in and around the country.

KEYWORDS

- **artificial intelligence**
- **e-finance**
- **smart phones**
- **mobile banking**
- **wealth technology**

REFERENCES

Allen, F. M. E-Finance: An Introduction. *J. Financ. Serv. Res.* **2002,** *22*, 5–27. https://doi.org/10.1023/A:1016007126394

Barkhordari, M.; Nourollah, Z.; Mashayekhi, H.; Mashayekhi, Y.; Ahangar, M. Factors Influencing Adoption of E-Payment Systems: An Empirical Study on Iranian Customers. *Inform. Syst. e-Busi. Manage.* **2016,** *15* (1), 89–116.

Citigroup. *Digital Disruption: How FinTech Is Forcing Banking to a Tipping Point*; Citigroup, 2016.

CrowdfundingHub. Current State of Crowdfunding in Europe: An Overview of the Crowdfunding Industry in More Than 25 Countries: Trends, Volumes & Regulations, Amsterdam: Crowdfunding Hub, 2016.

Glaser, F.; Zimmermann, K.; Haferkorn, M.; Weber, M.; Siering, M. Bitcoin—Asset or Currency? Revealing Users' Hidden Intentions. In Hileman, G., Rauchs, M. Global Cryptocurrency Benchmarking Study; Cambridge Centre for Alternative Finance: Cambridge, 2017.

Gomber, P. K. Digital Finance and FinTech: Current Research and Future Research Directions. *J. Busi. Econ.* **2017,** *87* (5), 537–580.

http://cashlessindia.gov.in/digital_payment_methods.html

https://www.bankbazaar.com/ifsc/digital-payment.html#10-Types-of-Digital-Payment-Methods-in-India

Innovate Finance, Innovate finance manifesto: UK 2020, Innovate Finance, 2015.

Kim, C.; Tao, W.; Shin, N.; Kim, K. An Empirical Study of Customers' Perceptions of Security and Trust in E-Payment Systems. *Electron. Com. Res. App.* **2010,** *9* (1), 84–95.

Kosba, A.; Miller, A.; Shi, E.; Wen, Z.; Papamanthou, C. Hawk: The Blockchain Model of Cryptography and Privacy-Preserving Smart Contracts. In Proceedings of the 2016 IEEE Symposium on Security and Privacy (SP), 2016.

Leong, K.; Sung, A. FinTech (Financial Technology): What is It and How to Use Technologies to Create Business Value in Fintech Way? *Int. J. Innov. Manage. Technol.* **2018,** *9* (2), 77.

Luther, W.; White, L. Can Bitcoin Become a Major Currency? *SSRN Electron. J.* **2014**.

McWaters, R. *The Future of Financial Services: How Disruptive Innovations Are Reshaping the Way Financial Services Are Structured, Provisioned and Consumed*; World Economic Forum, 2015.

Nicoletti, B. *The Future of FinTech*, 1st ed.; Palgrave Macmillan, 2017.

Pilkington, M. Blockchain Technology: Principles and Applications. In *Research Handbook on Digital Transformations*; Olleros, F., Zhegu, M., Eds., 2nd ed.; Edward Elgar: Montreal, 2016.

Proc. Twenty Second European Conference on Information Systems, Tel Aviv, 2014.

PwC, Financial services technology 2020 and beyond: Embracing Disruption, PwC, 2016.

Terekhova, M. Is Fintech Really Revolutionising UK Pension Schemes? Pensions Expert, 2016.

Wang, S.; Fan, J.; Zhang, M. An Empirical Study on the Impact of Perceived Benefit, Risk and Trust on E-Payment Adoption: Comparing Quick Pay and Union Pay in China. In Proceedings of the 2015 7th International Conference on Intelligent Human-Machine Systems and Cybernetics, 2015.

Zyskind, G.; Nathan, O.; Pentland, A. Decentralizing Privacy: Using Blockchain to Protect Personal Data. In Proceedings of the 2015 IEEE Security and Privacy Workshops, 2015.

CHAPTER 4

Fintech Retail Banking and Risk Management: Best Practices

ABHISHEK SINHA

Vigyan Jyoti Institute of Management, Hyderabad, India

ABSTRACT

Fintech has disrupted the way retail banks work in the last decade post-subprime crisis. This disruption has played an important role in propelling financial services to the next level. The innovations in the sector have made the financial services sector more customer-friendly and technologically enabled. However, in the retail banking space, disruption caused by Fintech has led to a challenging risk management environment. Risks of fraud, data theft, and technology risk have increased manifold. It is imperative to create an environment where risk management framework plays a critical role in reducing the overall risk and hence creates an ecosystem that helps establish more sustainable businesses. The chapter identifies the major risk elements and helps design a risk management framework that would enable companies to manage risk more efficiently in the system. If the Fintech companies fail to self-regulate, the regulations introduced by the financial services regulators across the globe may disrupt the innovations caused by the Fintech sector.

4.1 INTRODUCTION

The rate of change in the financial services industry has seen tremendous growth in the recent past. This change is driven by customers' demand

Revolutionary Challenges and Opportunities of Fintech. Shweta Anand, PhD, Shalini Srivastav, PhD, Vikas Garg, PhD, & Geetika Garg (Eds.)

for a hassle-free, digitalized experience without compromising with the security involved in such transactions. This has led to the evolution of a completely new industry—the FinTech industry.

FinTech is the short form for financial technology and denotes the adoption of technology for enhancing customer experience (Schueffel, 2016). In today's fast-tracked world where every customer is looking for a more convenient, customized and hassle-free experience, technological intervention at different points of the financial services value chain helps create a better experience for the customers. The financial technology hence is the next big disruption that would change the very way the financial services sector works.

This revolution has also brought about a paradigm change in the way retail banks operate. The retail banking business pertains to plain vanilla borrowing and lending of money. Traditionally, the rate of change in the sector was slow (Leong and Sung, 2018). These changes in the banking sector were driven by the need to decrease costs and increase profits. The customers were not the focus. However, Fintech has caused a demand-driven change in the very way the business works (Kotarba, 2016). Let us deep dive into how this process of change took place.

The Fintech revolution in the retail banking sector is to be impacted by the confluence of two unrelated events at the same time. The first incident impacted the customer's expectation from the retail banking sector. Increasing accessibility of the internet to retail customers and rising computer literacy across demographic profiles led to a change in product expectations (Buckley and Webster, 2016). In 1995, less than 0.5% of the world had access to the internet and by January 2020, three-fifth of the world had access to the internet according to International World Stats (Internationalworldstat.com).

At the same time, there was a drastic change in the way the banks looked at their customers. The Fintech revolution in retail banking started in 2008 at the peak of the financial crisis. Many banking sector employees were then thrown out of jobs. These ex-bankers had a fair understanding of how the banking sector worked and they started introducing Fintech products. Most of these products were built with the customers' experience as the outcome in mind and not cost reduction. These bankers were able to understand the demand and supply that existed in the digitized world. The same has been aptly captured in the following statement:

This unwavering client focus, in my opinion, makes a significant difference for all Fintech firms. Honestly, banks tend to be more concerned with how to provide new products and increase profits than with what customers desire. In light of this, it follows that if you asked customers if they wanted items like overdrafts, where they make the majority of their revenue, they would likely respond negatively. Therefore, FinTechs can approach it from a new perspective.

Both the events together led to the Fintech revolution that is being witnessed now. With the Fintech revolution, impacting the retail banking industry, the industry grew exponentially.

These Fintech companies are financed by private equity players who are not looking at short-term profits and hence, these firms have more flexibility. With more flexibility comes more risk. The strength of a financial services company to a great extent depends on its risk management process. The risk management process, on the other hand, depends on the regulatory requirements. The same applies to the Fintech sector. Hence, for a sector, such as a Fintech sector whose growth depends on the ability to innovate and disrupt regulations at times may act as a downside risk. Moreover, this industry was not regulated like how the banks were, and hence the advent of regulations to protect customers' interest is a challenge that could lead to the disruption of the sector.

According to experts, if the risk management system for a Fintech company does not evolve systemic risk would increase exponentially. This is because the popularity of the sector is increasing at an increasing rate. A lot of traditional banks across the globe are now embracing technology to compete with the smaller exclusive Fintech firms. Hence, this has led to the emergence of technology like an imminent source of risk.

To sum it up, managing risks and optimizing returns is of paramount importance to enable sustainable business models for Fintech companies which are leading the financial services revolution. The role of risk management to stem systemic risk becomes more critical as these organizations now gather momentum and scale-up.

4.2 CHANGING SCENARIO OF RETAIL BANKING

The above-mentioned advent of Fintech players has led to four basic changes in the way the retail banking sector functions. These changes have mandated a fresh look at the risk profile of companies operating in this sector. Firstly, most Fintech companies are focusing on different aspects of customers' needs rather than trying to be a one-shop stop to satisfy all the customer's needs at one time. In other words, there is an unbundling of services that are provided to customers. This leads to focused products that understand customer's needs better. Hence, there is the simplification of the products from the customer's perspective. These broaden the market as the choice for the client increases leading to a higher number of potential customers now availing the benefit of this sector. This has led to an overall increase in systemic risk.

Secondly, customers have now shifted to more digitalized financial platforms. The reason is that access to mobile internet has increased across the globe making it easier for customers to bank online using the internet connection on their mobile. Transferring money and making payments with a click of a button is in vogue. Hence, mobile now performs the same function which a branch performed a few years back. The technology risk has hence increased manifold.

Thirdly, a lot of entrepreneurs running Fintech start-ups are not from banking backgrounds, hence they may not be aware of the nuances of the banking sector. The culture of these banks is also different. They are less regulated and resemble that of a traditional software firm more than a traditional bank, hence impacting the functioning of the financial sector. There is a need to revisit the risk profile of the sector.

Fourthly, the customer is now hardly interacting with the banker. Hence, it is easier for customers to camouflage their identity. This makes innovative Fintech companies the first choice for customers who indulge in fraudulent business. Hence, the risk of banks increases multifold. There is an imminent risk of regulators increasing control on these banks leading to other customers being impacted.

4.3 RISKS RELATING TO FINTECH SECTOR

Fintech companies refer to those companies that bank primarily on technology. The technology sectors are ever-evolving, and hence the biggest challenge for the risk management team is to develop an understanding of the new technology that it brings to the fore along with the challenges in measuring the impact of the risk. Furthermore, because these Fintech companies are smaller in size, a lot of risks that may become tangible when the company grows may be ignored as of now. Thus, the process of identifying risk in the Fintech sector is going to be complex (Arner et al., 2016). This section identifies those risks.

4.3.1 ALTERNATIVE SOURCES OF FINANCING

The profitability of a retail bank primarily depends on its ability to raise money at a reasonable rate and then lend it at a higher rate to earn profits. Fintech companies that are innovative by nature look at various new methods of raising funds such as borrowing from the marketplace. Borrowing from the marketplace has played an important role in increasing financial inclusion and broadening the capital market. However, these loans may be riskier even though it may come at a higher cost. A lot of Fintech companies also tend to lend money to these marketplaces. Some of the risks such as data theft and money laundering can impact the reputation of the banking sector in general.

If these banks are such that the risk is transferred to the final consumer, the risk of the retail consumer increases rather than decreasing. Case in the point is Lending Club. It started operations in 2006 intending to cause business disruption. The company promised a fixed interest rate payment which was higher than the return on plain vanilla bonds. This led to banks and Fintech companies investing in marketplace lenders. More than four-fifth of the loan was being financed from financial institutions including Fintech companies and hedge funds.

4.3.2 ROLE OF ARTIFICIAL INTELLIGENCE IN FINANCIAL ADVISORY SERVICES

With the advent of technology, in the process of investment decision-making, customers are now subject to more unbiased views provided through Robo advisory services. The views do not suffer from any human behavior traits which at times undermine the interest of the clients. However, there is always a risk of technology failure. These are low-frequency high-value risks which are often ignored by the Fintech companies. Such risks lead to reputation risks and may cause a huge impact on the future growth of the financial institution if not handled properly. The risk is higher for retail banks that cater to high net worth individuals (Jung et al., 2019).

Moreover, there is a possibility that Robo Advisory fails to identify the unique needs of the customers as pointed out by experts. It also leads to "investor disengagement." This would impact clients at the time when the markets are highly volatile and have entered the uncharted area. Hence, Robo advisory without the involvement of financial planners may not be advisable.

4.4 DATA SECURITY

For traditional banks, the ability to maintain the confidentiality of data was primarily the function of the integrity of employees, and time data integrity is now a function of the robustness of the information technology security system that protects the data online. The same can be attributed to increasing online transactions. The incidence of online data thefts has increased exponentially. Data sharing by banks with third parties Fintech companies also lead to a higher level of risk. The security breach at the third-party end can also do irreparable damage to the financial system. Developing countries, such as Brazil and South Africa have seen quite a few instances of such cases. Hackers are coming up with new ways to breach data security. Moreover, customers are sensitive to their financial data being shared as it may lead to irreparable financial damage for these companies (Lee and Shin, 2018).

4.5 INCREASING INCIDENCE OF FAILURE TO DETECT FRAUD

Risk intelligent Fintech companies are few. Hence, processes that are technology-driven and require fewer instances of human intervention many times have a higher level of opaqueness about them. In other words, there are more instances of the right arm not knowing what the left arm is doing. This may lead to the risk of fraud not being detected for long, leading to huge losses. The companies do not have a proper strategy to identify and measure risk at the time of innovation. Hence, these innovation-driven companies are more prone to falter in preventing the incidence of fraud if they do not become risk intelligently.

The companies should, for instance, have a standard operating procedure for using client data. There are instances of regulatory breaches because of a lack of understanding of the importance of not sharing the client data with other departments within the organization (Funston and Wagner, 2010).

4.6 PAYMENT GATEWAYS

Technology-driven payment gateways have now dominated the retail banking space. In other words, the success of the banking system depends completely on the risk management of payment gateways. Payment gateways are subject to the following risks:

a. Encryption Risk

The data has not been encrypted properly. The cost of data encryption may be high so many times a Fintech company may choose to encrypt only those data which it deems sensitive. This causes an overall increase in the riskiness of the business model (Aldridge and Krawciw, 2017).

b. DDOS Attacks

These types of hackers-induced attacks involve flooding the server with excessive data to reduce the internet speed resulting in poor productivity and performance. It also impacts the customer's satisfaction level. The impact can be in the form of disrupting digital processes or leading to the damage of hardware.

c. Data Breach

Data breaches generally rise due to a problem with the encryption process. If the encryption process is not robust, there is a possibility of a data breach. Hence, to prevent data breach, it is important to encrypt the data that are being used.

d. Fraud Risks

Payment gateways are susceptible to fraud risks. Fraud risks along with security risks are the most common risks associated with third-party payment processors. In the case of the fraud risks, there is a huge reputational risk that the company faces (Begenau et al., 2015).

4.7 AMBIGUITY IN REGULATORY NORMS

The regulatory norms on Fintech companies are ambiguous and hence create risks for business entities operating in the space. There is a likelihood of a tightening of the norm in the future. This could result in discouraging innovation in the future and hence the very foundation of Fintech can be impacted by the ambiguity in regulatory norms. Hence, according to experts, this could disrupt the future and may lead to increased downside risk. Leading traditional banks may be wary of working with Fintech companies. Subsequently, customer-centric innovation may impact the banking sector, thus, ambiguity in the regulatory norm may be dealt with by governments to reduce the systemic risk in the sector (Buchak et al., 2018).

4.8 PEOPLE RISK

Financial service companies primarily deal with the money of others. Hence, there is a high level of risk involved in both traditional as well as Fintech models. However, the level of risk associated with Fintech is higher as there is a lesser number of employees and most of the checks and balances are automated. If these checks and balances are manipulated, then there is a possibility of risk management failure. Hence, people are one of the most important assets of any Fintech company. The resoluteness of people to make the system robust is of prima facie importance in the Fintech space (Chishti and Barberis, 2016).

Secondly, to ensure continuity of processes, it is important to arrest attrition in the company. In other words, the inability to reduce attrition can lead to people risk in this kind of organization.

4.9 OPERATIONAL RISK

Retail banking Fintech companies are rapidly evolving operations to make them more flexible and agile. These firms are primarily driven by an urge to be innovative, but the same can increase the riskiness of the business model.

Capital expenditure on regulatory frameworks that banks have been conspicuous by its absence for the Fintech sector. The company is also low on the number of employees.

The culture of the firm may be impacted by these flaws in process robustness; for instance, lax controls in the finance department may give rise to theft or fraud. Employee litigation and reputational harm are two possible effects in human resources (Romnova and Kudinska, 2016).

4.10 TECHNOLOGICAL RISK

Fintech companies are primarily driven by technology and hence the technological risk cannot be ignored. Technological risk refers to the risk related to the failure of technology. These financial institutions bank on the latest technological innovation. There is always a possibility of technological failure if the technology in question is not tested and robust. To ensure proper testing of technology, a framework for testing technology being employed needs to be drafted. This document should also provide for ensuring that technology does not fail during stressed economic or political times. Many traditional banks customarily were averse to moving to advanced technology, however, with the Fintech revolution, most banks are now relying on the latest technological innovations. This has made technological risk more systemic (Listyo et al., 2018).

Chime, a leading challenger bank that is completely digital had more than 5 million customers in October 2019. The bank had to face customer wrath and loss of reputation when it faced a power outage and was not able to provide services to 5 million of its employees in 2019. The glitch was caused due to technological snag at the end of Galileo Financials a Fintech company that provided backend technological support to the bank.

4.11 FINANCIAL MARKET DISRUPTIONS

Fintech sector came into existence because customers were not happy with the financial services sector in terms of technology and services. Hence, the major impact of Fintech innovation is disruption. Thus, existing Fintech companies always face the risk of being obsolete in terms of the services rendered and the technology used on the advent of new players. The risk at the time is unpredictable and hence difficult to gauge.

The following are the major disruptions caused by the Fintech sector in retail space:

Automated chatting helps:

A lot of Fintech companies use automated chat helps. These chatbots leverage artificial intelligence and could continuously improve its performance through its interaction with the customers of the bank. Thus, innovation has helped banks and financial services reduce their fixed costs considerably. The efficiency of services also increases at times where the support team is not motivated to answer the questions being asked, and their rude behavior impacts customer attrition adversely.

Machine learning and fraud detection:

One of the major disruptions that have been caused by Fintech companies in the retail space is the detection of frauds with the help of machine learning and artificial intelligence. This has helped retail banks reduce their risks substantially.

The disruption caused in the brick and mortar banks:

With digital banks being preferred by the customers and reducing fixed operating costs for banks, traditional banks have also started increasing their online banking presence and this has impacted the rate of disruption (Magnuson, 2018).

4.12 CONTAGION RISK

It refers to the risk that the impact of the failure of one Fintech company may have a systemic impact on all the other Fintech companies. Fintech companies have become an integral part of the whole financial service system. In the retail banking segment, they are playing a very important role presently. However, the rate of innovation in the sector makes them vulnerable to unexpected losses or losses they are not covered for. In the event of contagion, this may impact all the other Fintech companies too. Hence, regulatory norms should be strong enough to prevent such occurrences from happening in the future.

4.13 CREATING A RISK MANAGEMENT FRAMEWORK

Fintechs are an important part of the financial system. They are partnering with the traditional banks in all spheres of retail banking. Some of the risks, such as data theft and money laundering can impact the reputation of the banking sector in general.

Their vulnerabilities could hence impact the economies of the country where they operate. Therefore, the systemic risk needs to be stymied by creating a framework to manage risk for Fintech companies. Following are the steps involved in creating a risk framework for the Fintech sector:

4.14 CORPORATE GOVERNANCE

The success of any strategic endeavor to a great extent is hinged on the intent of the senior management. In the case of Fintech companies whose model is based on the ability to create business disruption and risk-taking, it becomes even more relevant (Mok and Saha, 2017). The management's intent to create a long-term sustainable business instead of creating short-term business model is what drives risk management initiatives. It has often been seen that senior management may be interested in profitability. However, it is the role of the independent directors to drive home the importance of risk management to prevent agency type 1 errors.

Following are some of the steps that can be taken by the board of director to ensure risk management success:

4.15 APPOINTING A CHIEF RISK OFFICER

It has often been seen that Fintech companies which are traditionally low on personnel, end up appointing employees with the additional role of managing risk. This approach will not work as the delineation of risk function with operations is of prima facie importance to ensure the independence of the function. The risk for a Fintech company working on retail banking aspects can arise from two sources—technology and retail banking. Hence, the Chief Risk Officer should understand both technology and banking function at a Fintech company to do justice to his role (Lam, 2001).

Merely appointing a Chief Risk Officer often is not enough. It is important to ensure that the risk manager has enough autonomy to make decisions. This depends on the reporting structure that the company has. Best practices mandate that the chief risk officer should report directly to the board of directors and not to the senior management. This is to reduce the incidence of agency problems type 1 and type 2 in building a sustainable risk management model (Taleb and Pilpel, 2004).

4.16 APPOINTING A RISK COMMITTEE

To underline the importance of risk, the board of directors needs to form a risk committee. The risk committee can ideally be chaired by a director who is an expert on risk management and has a fair knowledge of the technology being used by the company (Al Hadi et al., 2016). He should also be acquainted with the regulatory requirements and best practices being followed globally. In the absence of such a board of directors, it should be chaired by the chairman of the board of directors.

It should have representation from all the functional areas. The members must have a firm understanding of the risk management function and believe in the philosophy of building a risk intelligent organization.

The main function of the risk committee would include:

a. Defining the Risk Appetite of the Organization

The first and foremost role of the risk committee is to define the risk appetite of the organization. The same needs to be done with the consultation of senior management and the board of directors. The level of risk the company undertakes should be consistent with the long-term organizational goals. The risk appetite of the Fintech company in retail banking space may be very different from the risk appetite of a traditional bank. A Fintech company, due to its structure and private equity funding, can absorb a lot more risk than other players in the financial service sector. However, these risks must be managed properly to build a more sustainable business model. The sole objective of having a risk management function is to understand the risks that exist and keep them under control. The same can be achieved only if the organization is aware of its risk appetite.

b. Confirming all Risks Have Been Defined

The risk committee needs to ensure that all risks have been identified. For a Fintech company catering to the banking sector, the challenge is to understand the changes that the company is making in terms of business model and technology. The implication of these changes on the risk metrics of the Fintech company must be measured objectively and quantified wherever possible to estimate the change in risk levels if any. The complexity of managing risk in a Fintech company comes from the high level of automation and hence leads to an increased level of opaqueness in the organization. Fintech companies are more prone to "unexpected loss" than their traditional counterparts because of their unconventional nature of business. Thus, it is of paramount importance to identify all the risks.

c. Defining and Measuring Risk Consistently Across the Organization

To ensure that the risk is consistent with the risk appetite of the organization, accuracy in risk management is an important parameter. Hence, to define and measure the enterprise wise risk consistency in the measurement of risk is imperative. Therefore, the company should make efforts to measure risk consistently. The same can be done if the definition of risk is shared with the operational managers regularly. Operational managers then must vet the definition of risks as defined by the risk team. The failure of operational managers in understanding the definition and nature of risk can lead to two different problems. Firstly, risks can be underestimated. In such cases, as has been evidenced during the subprime crisis of 2008 in the U.S. it is like a ticking time bomb ready to explode. Secondly, risks may be overestimated this would lead to a higher cost in terms of managing risks that do not exist for the business entity. The same will impact the profitability of the company and hence valuations in the stock markets will be affected adversely. The risk committee should thus ensure that the risks are defined accurately and have the same connotation for different arms of the organization. With a lot of Fintech companies having a scalable model, it becomes inevitable to ensure consistency in risk management definition.

d. Developing the Risk Management Strategy

To build a sustainable model for risk-taking, it is important to have a risk management strategy document in place. This document should be prepared by the risk management team, vetted by the risk management committee, and ratified by the senior management. The document should provide a guiding light for everyone in the organization on how the various risks ought to be dealt with. Risks can either be accepted, avoided, transferred, or mitigated. The whole organization should have a similar view of dealing with defined risks. Objectivity in dealing with risk is very important to strategize a sustainable growth model for the company. The framework for dealing with risk should involve views of operational managers and risk management experts. In the case of Fintech companies, views of technology experts and regulatory experts also are of paramount importance.

e. Outsourcing Decisions

It is pertinent to understand that the company cannot develop expertise in all aspects of risk management. Hence, it is prudent for a Fintech company to outsource the part of risk management in which they may not be able to develop competencies. The decision should come from the top. The role of the risk management committee in deciding the same is of paramount importance. A lot of companies prefer to develop competencies in those areas which are critical to the survival of the company, for instance, managing liquidity and regulatory risk.

Outsourcing of risk management function can help increase the efficiency of the processes and can also lead to cost optimization. However, there should be an in-house capability to assess the major risks and plan strategies to face the risks better. Regulatory norms are to have adhered and the assurance of the same must be taken by the in-house risk management team.

f. Defining the Feedback Loop

The success of the risk management system depends on its ability to learn from the mistakes and lapses in the past hence developing a strong feedback loop is an important source for the company to strengthen its risk management system. The feedback loop's effectiveness is contingent on the involvement of the senior management and the board of directors in the process of evaluating the results obtained from the risk management process. In case there is a divergence from accepted norms, the same should be brought to the notice of the risk management committee. The reasons for divergence need to be investigated and ways of plugging the systemic failure should be developed. A road map for future risk management strategy should depend on the success of the present strategies in place.

Funston, F.; Wagner, S. *Surviving and Thriving in Uncertainty: Creating the Risk Intelligent Enterprise*; John Wiley & Sons, 2010.

https://www.computerworld.com/article/3427766/what-are-the-biggest-risks-fintech-poses-to-banks-.html

Internationalworldstat.com

Jung, D.; Glaser, F.; Köpplin, W. Robo-Advisory: Opportunities and Risks for the Future of Financial Advisory. In *Advances in Consulting Research*; Springer: Cham, 2019; pp 405–427.

Kotarba, M. New Factors Inducing Changes in the Retail Banking Customer Relationship Management (CRM) and Their Exploration by the FinTech Industry. *Foundations Manage.* **2016,** *8* (1), 69–78.

Lam, J. The CRO Is Here to Stay. *Risk Manage.* **2001,** *48* (4), 16–16.

Lee, I.; Shin, Y. J. Fintech: Ecosystem, Business Models, Investment Decisions, and Challenges. *Busi. Horiz.* **2018,** *61* (1), 35–46.

Leong, K.; Sung, A. FinTech (Financial Technology): What Is It and How To Use Technologies to Create Business Value in Fintech Way? *Int. J. Innov. Manage. Technol.* **2018,** *9* (2), 74–78.

Listyo, P.; Fernando, E.; Savina, G.; Tirtamulia, L. M. Technology Risk in Financial Technology at Online Transportation Systems. In *2018 International Conference on Information Management and Technology (ICIMTech)*; IEEE, Sept 2018; pp 149–154.

Magnuson, W. Regulating Fintech. *Vand. L. Rev.* **2018,** *71*, 1167.

Mok, A.; Saha, R. Strategic Risk Management in Banking. *Deloitte Inside Magaz.*, 2017.

Romnova, I.; Kudinska, M. *Banking and Fintech: A Challenge or an Opportunity? Contemporary Issues in Finance: Current Challenges from Across Europe*; Emerald Group Publishing Limited, 2016.

Schueffel, P. Taming the Beast: A Scientific Definition of Fintech. *J. Innov. Manage.* **2016,** *4* (4), 32–54.

Taleb, N. N.; Pilpel, A. On the Unfortunate Problem of the Nonobservability of the Probability Distribution. Unpublished Manuscript, 2004. http;//www. fooledbyrandomness. com/ knowledge. pdf (accessed June 7, 2006).

Wu, Y. T. FinTech Innovation and Anti-Money Laundering Compliance. *NTU L. Rev.* **2017,** *12*, 201.

CHAPTER 5

Fintech Startups Challenges and Suggested Strategies to Overcome

TEENA HASSIJA, SWATI WATTS, and MONIKA GOEL

Institute of Research and Studies, Faridabad, India

ABSTRACT

In the present time, almost every country is swamped in fighting with the unemployment or underemployment phenomenon. The global competitive environment compels the youth to focus on generating self-employment sources and be their boss. Unemployment is one of the biggest problems in our country as 70% of the Indian population is youth and there is an alarming situation to look upon the solutions to this problem. The most promising solution to this problem could be self-employed and develop an entrepreneurship and startup culture in India. To develop a culture, the Indian government has fostered many schemes and policies. Support of the government is venerable as it covers almost every aspect to make the startup successful. Apart from gigantic support and policies provided by the Indian government; the new startups are facing many challenges and facing many difficulties for their survival. The common challenges which are faced by almost every new startup in India like lack of funds, high legal requirements/regulations, lack of managerial/business skills, lack of innovative technologies, excessive cost as being a small unit, lack of know-how, and global competition.

Revolutionary Challenges and Opportunities of Fintech. Shweta Anand, PhD, Shalini Srivastav, PhD, Vikas Garg, PhD, & Geetika Garg (Eds.)

The present chapter is an attempt to discuss various challenges being faced by Fintech startups in India as they are the future of the economy. The growth of Fintech startups directly leads to economic development.

Financial sectors including traditional banking channels are essentially adopting technology for its survival and growth. Fintech companies are financial service providers and make all the deliveries through innovative technologies. There is no doubt in saying that Fintech is marking rapid growth at the global level and India is also adopting the Fintech services wholeheartedly. The present chapter is focusing on the role of Fintech startups in filling the gap of financial inclusions and what the various challenges being faced by them. This chapter also tried well to develop the strategies which may ensure the sustainability and growth of the sector.

The role of the incubator sector is very essential in promoting Fintech startups in India. Business incubators help in facing the various kinds of challenges and also provides many facilities, such as venture capital, funds, and corrective measures to increase the profits.

5.1 INTRODUCTION

The launch of Digital India moment in 2015 along with technology has played an important role in transforming our payment interface. In the last 5–10 years, the citizens of India or individuals who were hesitant about the online payment services have changed their minds. A large proportion of the population has changed the ways of transactions. So, innovation and technology have together brought a drastic change in the traditional financial sector. Technological advancements have encouraged the new-age Fintech players who are challenging the traditional models. Fintech companies got a good start or we can say that demonetization in 2016 kick-started these new-age companies. If we are going to see the data dated May 07, 2020, India holds cumulative digital transaction of $81, 197 million at a 25.3% YoY with over 553.7 million registered users online (https://timesnext.com/10-most-successful-fintech-startups-companies-in-india/) India is also one of the leading startup hubs in the world, followed by the United Kingdom, Singapore, and Germany. The recent lockdown has given these companies a boost as Indian digital payments have suddenly and significantly grown. And most importantly, convenience along with security has been the mantra for the growth of digital payments.

5.2 MEANING OF FINTECH STARTUPS

The term Fintech has been derived from two words "Finance" and "Technology" So, the term itself says that we are adding two important fields, that is, finance plus technology. Fintech refers to a system where we are merging the new technological trends with finance to provide better financial services to the clients in the form of transactions and digital payments. The major role of Fintech is to swap traditional methods with modern ones. Fintech is a dynamic industry that is growing day by day. Consequently, there are various ways to define Fintech. For a variety of reasons, the definition provided below pleased us for this chapter:

> Fintechs are fast-growing companies that combine cutting-edge business models and cutting-edge technologies to allow, improve, and disrupt the financial services industry.
>
> –Prof. Chuen and Teo

This definition includes startups, mature companies, and even nonfinancial companies working in the digital financial space.

In 2007, Fintech starts up took a major step by offering digital mobile recharges. Increasing trends of smart mobile phones and digital channels gave them a good response. As a result, by 2010, India launched its first real-time payment system "IMPS," and then in 2016, it introduced "UPI." The traditional cash-driven Indian economy is taking a step back as Fintech companies have the potential to give transparent services and also have the advantage of the convenience of time.

Some key growth drivers make the Fintech industry a hit. Some of them are the following:

- High usage of smart mobile phones (around 12 billion mobile subscribers till 2019).
- Growing disposable income.
- A huge number of people enroll in Aadhar Yojana.
- High level of banking usage by Jan Dhan yojana.

If we are going to talk about key segments within Fintech space, it includes:

- Digital payments
- Digital lending's

- Bank Technology
- Insurance Technology
- Wealth Technology

In all the above segments, India is witnessing the birth of startups with innovative technologies. There are around 400 payments startups in the country. The urban population is getting dependent on Fintech companies to save time and also to avoid heavy documentation whereas the rural population is also getting the advantage of time and also long distances which they use to travel for financial institutions. The key areas where these companies are having the next wave of innovations are Robo advisory, digital payments, block chain, drones, machine learning, and artificial intelligence.

5.3 FUTURE OF FINTECH STARTUPS

The services sector is one of the leading sectors in India's GDP, as it contributes 54.17% of India's Gross Value Added at the current price in 2018–2019 (https://www.ibef.org/industry/services.aspx). According to Guile and Quinn (1988); (Fitzsimmons and Fitzsimmons, 2008), the service sector plays its vital role in an economy as it is an essential part of the economy. Once we talk about the service sector, the predominant sector is financial services. Nowadays, financial service has started shifting from traditional face-to-face transactions to the E-finance domain. Lee and Shin (2018) defined E-financial as "all forms of financial services, such as banking, insurance, and stock trading performed through electronic means, including the internet and World Wide Web." Thus, digital financial services provide access to accounts, and other financial services at the platform of people's choice, they do not have to visit any firm or bank.

India is widely accepting of the digital transmission of the financial system. According to a report shared by IBEF in 2019 that India has registered 3133 core digital transactions in the financial year 2019 which is expected to rise to 1527 crores in FY20 (till September 2019). (https://www.ibef.org/industry/financial-services-india.aspx). Lee and Shin (2018) With the remarkable growth of digital financing in India, Fintech enterprises are also growing at a rapid speed. Fintechs are reassuring to the financial industry a promising growth and returns by improving the quality of financial services, cutting costs, and by building a more assorted and secure "Financial Land-Scale" ("The FinTech Revolution," 2015).

In the global paradigm, the Fintech startups envelop several consumer-facing services of the Financial significance. In a practical situation, Fintech startups are not in a very good condition. Many of the startups collapse even before the start of their functioning. There is a requirement for development to startups to ensure economic development and growth. Gazel and Schwienbacher (2020) examined over 972 Fintech startups located in France from 2000 to July 2018 and the researchers found that 122 startups already existed in the market, they could not even start their business. PwC (2016) also reported that 83% of worldwide fintech startups are at risk.

Now, the time has come to shelter the Fintech startups and the government should make some protective regulations to secure the sector. Colombelli et al. (2016) sturdily supported for the formation and survival of innovative startups and it should be one major agenda of the economic policy of every country.

5.4 CHALLENGES FOR FINTECH STARTUPS IN INDIA

India is the second-largest Fintech startup base in the world followed by the USA. More than 1100 Fintech companies including startups are working at present. The Indian Fintech sector is primarily involved in three services as digital lending, digital payments, and wealth management. Apart from the unremarkable success of the sector, the sector is still facing some challenges, which could be considered as opportunities for the Fintech.

5.5 REGULATORY FACTORS

To deal with regulation is a daily task for every kind of business. The pressure is a little high globally on the Fintech startups due to their nature of the business.

The rules and regulations made and imposed by government or government agencies have a strong influence on the startups. The success and failure of a newly established business are largely dependent on the regulatory environment. It is very much required to understand the major regulations every business may have to go with. Registration is required for every business if you wish to start as a company or LLP. If a new startup wants to take support under a government scheme, they may have to go through with a very tedious legal documentations and long process. On the other side, registration as a company or a startup provides recognition to the newborn and they can create loyalty among customers. Other government schemes relating to trade practices, taxes, import tariffs, fiscal policies, monetary policies, etc. also affect startups. But it is again a difficult task for maintenance of the records and meets the standards to avail of the benefits of the scheme. The scheme seems very attractive but not easy to avail in a single go. The government also has provided many other reliefs and benefits to startups like. In case the government provides benefits for exportation, then again, it may be difficult for a startup to meet international demand.

These government regulations restrict the activities of Fintechs or impose extra financial load which again is a hefty task for new establishments to afford. The authors have exemplified a few of them like restrictions imposed on Fintech insurance service providers is much higher as compared with any other country, which can be easily identified by comparing global benchmarking of regulations applicable to such firms. A comparative analysis of the restrictions applicable to the Fintech insurance firms across the world is incorporated by "Steering Committee" constitutes under Department of Economic Affairs, Ministry of Finance in their report on Fintech-related issues shared in 2019. The report clearly stated that Fintech insurance sector is not able to execute well since Indian government has restricted the sector to do advertisement, to share reviews, rating, to deal in noninsurance products, third-party dealing, whereas all these working conditions are permissible in all the other developed countries as USA, UK, France, Germany, and Japan and so on.

(https://dea.gov.in/sites/default/files/Report%20of%20the%20Steering%20Committee%20on%20Fintech_1.pdf)

Regulations are not limited to the imposition of restrictions rather these companies have to take the license from many different authorities and have to maintain their website interface according to the guidelines provided. Chug (2020) mentioned in his paper that the insurance Fintechs are obliged to follow the regulations provided by the IRDA (Insurance Web Aggregators) Regulations, 2017, and an annual fee of Rs. 50,000 is charged by the authority as aggregator charges.

Another very appealing example is Peer-to-Peer (P2P) lending by NBFC is followed by RBI directions and restricted to perform as an intimidator only. Moreover, these NBFCs are required to get registered with RBI and be certificated, and they have to report to RBI about Credit Information Companies. The appointment of "Nodal Officers" under the Ombudsman Scheme is also mandatory for these firms. Once we talk about the payments sector, which carries most innovative Fintech startups in India. To become a payment Fintech as Airtel Money, Paytm, etc. one has to take authority from RBI, have to hold many licenses for mobile banking, RTGS membership, IMPS, UPI along the regulations provided by National Payments Corporation of India (NPCI).

The Asset Management Companies (AMCs) are executed on the regulations of SEBI. This Fintech must be registered with SEBI and are advised to implement a separate direct plan for direct investment without involving any distributor. The other most restricted Fintech sector is blockchain and crypto currency, which is banned by RBI in 2018 and the final hearing is underway with SC. Hileman and Rauchs (2017) refereed four basic activities covered by blockchain activities as miners, crypto exchanges, payments, and Wallets, out of which miners.

5.6 ECONOMIC ENVIRONMENT

Businesses usually nurture well within favorable economic environments, whereas, a bad economic environment may hamper businesses and may not even allow starting. Thus, it is foremost important for every startup to deeply investigate the economic environment and predict accordingly. The predictions should be made in focusing all the vagueness. The major business decisions at micro and macro levels as the location of the business, type of business, price, director's composition, skilled labor, work culture, and policy segmentation and many like should have the flexibility to adjust with the fast-changing economic environment. As being uncontrollable environment, macro factors are more responsible for the success or failure of a new enterprise, which may include government policies and regulations, natural disasters, pandemics, market demand, competition, customer adaptability, and so on, whereas the microenvironment is adjusted according to the macro environment. The demand generation and raising customer adaptability to an unfamiliar service, on which they cannot trust fully, is a tedious task. For example, Fintech got huge familiarity in India at the time of demonetization in 2018 and then in 2020 during the period of COVID-19, where people are compelled to move to digital mode of finance.

5.7 VAST COMPETITION

Fintech startups must stay an eagle eye on key revolutionary developments in the industry. Every business needs to have surveillance for its survival and growth. When we talk about Fintech, completion is very vast and diagonal. Fintechs have competitions in themselves, with large and small-scale banks and even with other nonbanking firms. The competition for the startups is too vast they are not only competing with existing financial giants, such as Citi, Paytm, Google Pay, or PayPal, but the industry is catching the attention of many other big/small financial enterprises. Nonfinancial enterprises also have started moving toward this industry, such as trading e-commerce companies like Amazon Inc., telecommunication companies as Airtel money.

Fintechs mainly deal with online financial services, which primarily include borrowings, payments, and UPIs. All the banks and other NBOs are also providing their services by digital mode. In this scenario, the Fintech startups should have to be more cautious and strategic. Market improbability is frequent and universal for the financial sector, which may affect more new establishments and may become a cause of their failure. Once we talk about money, most of the Indians still hesitate in using Fintech services for their financial operations (https://razorpay.com/learn/fintech-startups-challenges-solutions/). In this state of affairs, it is the biggest challenge for the Fintech to convert people from traditional banking to an unfamiliar setup. Moreover, cyber financial crimes have made it more difficult for new birds to take off. It is very tough to gain faith and loyalty among Indian customers. The only mantra to sustain and develop is to provide transparent and superior quality services. Follow-up with the customers and good customer assistance can also work incalculably.

5.8 GAINING VENTURE CAPITAL

Startups across the world are famished with funds. It is never being easy for them to raise venture capital especially for Fintech startups. The business model of Fintech is not so familiar to every investor, so it is difficult to make them understand the major financial products and strategies of the business. Most of the time a new startup is lacking a skilled and experienced management team and they are not able to explicate the eminence and supremacy of their products and services and the differentiated technology being used in the business. Hence, these startups usually fail in convincing investors. The venture capitalist may also be interested in some more issues, including objectives of the business, prospective risks to the business, capital structure, startups intellectual property, return on investment, and so on.

In the case of Fintech startup which is competent enough to solve investor queries, then the chances to raise funds become a little high. The Fintech should attract the right strategic investor who has experience of investing for startups, so that the investor will be in a position to understand the inclusive risk. Apart from risk absorption, the experienced venture capitalist may also support the new birds in developing their market edges, product development, handling the regulatory issues, and drafting other strategies. In this scenario, the Fintech startups should have to take care of the contracts they are making with the investors, it may not become the biggest risk of losing their ownership, or investors may not take the control over the management.

5.9 MARKETING STRATEGIES

One of the major challenges could be faced by any new business set-up is customer acquisition. Undoubtedly, Fintechs are dealing online and there is no personal interaction among customers and the organization. Thus, it is more difficult for these enterprises to spread their business and have wider customer connectivity. There are many ways to connect with prospective customers and grab the lead, such as advertisements on famous search engines have a smart social media plan, build a high-quality website, and share attractive articles. All the media tools carry huge costs and new startups are already starving of funds. So, it may not be cumbersome for these companies. It is a big challenge for the Fintechs to select draft marketing strategies. They should create an appropriate and flexible budget for advertisement not to hinder the profits. A few things should be taken care of while making marketing strategies, such as the development of easy, apparent, and with a featured call-to-action fintech app, selection of social media networking, which is comparatively a cheap source of advertisement among all. Significant content may help in developing faith and trust in a very new system and trust is fundamental for sales above all the sale of financial products and services (https://www.digitalauthority.me/resources/fintech-marketing-strategies/).

5.10 ADVANCED TECHNOLOGIES AND INNOVATIONS

The main asset with the Fintech companies is their intellectual property and technologies they are using. In the present time, technologies are shifting very quickly and the existing technologies become either obsolete or need frequent updates. To survive in the market and to gain competitive advantage, the Fintech companies ought to center on the technology they are using. For the sustainability and growth in global markets, it is very much important to be the owner of a crime/hacking proof, a customer-oriented website, or a mobile application. For the safety concern, Fintech should implement "reasonable" technological safety measures which must be conformed to all the regulations and standards. The main focus should be on authentication, asset management, antivirus software, encryption, access controls, network monitoring, etc. On the other side, cost-effectiveness is a parallel challenge for beginners. Hence, technology selection is the key to success, so should be chosen wisely.

5.11 STRATEGIES TO OVERCOME THE CHALLENGES FACING BY FINTECH STARTUPS

For the last decade, Fintech startups across the country have shown convincingly that Indian startups in this sector are both innovative and technically viable. Fintech interventions have solved many problems of Banks, NBFCs, mutual funds, and insurance sectors. However, it is equally typical to see newly established Fintech businesses struggle to meet their operating expenses and turn a profit. It has been determined from the debate in the paper that technology by itself is insufficient to unlock the business's economic potential. A Fintech can become more lucrative and sustainable by having access to markets, knowledge of the newest technology, skill upgrades, design inputs, and a variety of other business development services. Major obstacles that prohibit such businesses from obtaining the best price for their goods include a lack of economies of scale, a weak marketing infrastructure, the absence of value addition, a lack of access to market knowledge, and a lack of organized purchasers. The choice of commercial activity and low sustainability is also caused by planning, marketing tactics, and a general lack of business strategy among entrepreneurs. Many of the strategies—particularly coping strategies, which are reactive responses to it.

5.12 INNOVATIVE CO-CREATION AND APPROPRIATE PARTNERSHIPS

The success of any business initiative is determined by its sustainability and income generated and not necessarily by technology intervention. Fintech startups should not only be best as technology breakthroughs but also as best service providers. Innovative co-creation and appropriate partnerships can add economic value to the innovation contributed by such enterprises. It can provide solutions that will make business more efficient, competitive, and inclusive and can simultaneously impact its sustainability positively. Partners of such enterprises need to graduate from the thought process of being technology providers to business solution providers if they have to create an enterprise.

Promoting partnerships among technology providers, investors, and key employees can ensure the sustainability of the business. However, because partners come from diverse backgrounds and occasionally have conflicting viewpoints, complicated cooperative procedures are frequently involved in partnerships. The Partnership approach should be some sort of official or informal agreement among the stakeholders who cooperate for a common goal and contribute to decision-making, planning, and resource allocation to share associated rewards and risks. The following are the main advantages of inventive co-creation and sensible alliances:

(i) Access to improved and more convenient facilities as well as a raised and stable income should be included among the benefits for technology suppliers.
(ii) The investor will gain from increased market size, more revenue, and a sense of social duty.

(iii) Benefits to key employees should include ensuring a better quality of life with job insecurity.

5.13 AN INTEGRATED APPROACH

A Fintech startup requires an integrated approach in terms of backward linkages with technology and forward linkages with the market. Some of the preliminary steps to be considered before launching a business are

(i) A primary survey of the local market and competitor analysis is to be conducted to understand the demand pattern.
(ii) The supply possibilities are to be ascertained by surveying the availability of different skills, infrastructure, and support services available.
(iii) Analysis of supply and demand area should be a microplanning exercise to be conducted so that scientific selection of business activities is ensured.
(iv) Entrepreneurs already pursuing the activity should be interviewed to understand the problems they faced and the solutions they have evolved.
(v) The data thus gathered should be analyzed and a business plan with detailed and practical implementation strategy to be devised.

5.14 BUSINESS DEVELOPMENT REQUIRES MORE THAN JUST TECHNOLOGY

The flaw in Fintech Startup is it starts and ends with technology. Fintech is not just about technology. It is also about creating a business plan, building capacity to implement that technology, and bring about a change. Such startups require considerable hand-holding in the areas of input supply, training, technical support, and market linkages. They also require enterprise development services and institutional development services though not necessarily in that order. Business Incubators and Accelerators working in the Fintech domain can play an important role in discovering sustainable business models built around the businesses they work with. They can prepare the ground for change, design programs that overcome the cultural resistance to become a business enterprise.

The focus of Fintech should shift from a technology-led approach to a market-led approach. In all new Fintech initiatives, both technical and nontechnical team members should visit and interact with market players before starting or expanding the business. To retain proper business relationships with customers' enterprises should maintain service quality and timely delivery. By being a service provider in a niche area, a Fintech can offer value-added outsourcing support to the established businesses which may choose them for internal lack of pace and infrastructure. The outsourcing services model offers opportunities to create win-win business models between the market players. Mobilizing and motivating the Fintech enterprises to emerge as group-based enterprises is an essential component in creating a sustainable business.

5.15 SELF-RELIANCE OR EQUITY DILUTION

The self-funding or bootstrapping approach solves a very small part of business finance. It particularly focuses on managing the cash flows of immediate concern for basic survival. The transformation of businesses requires some investments. With the focus on a business model, the Fintech startups can approach for financial support of various agencies, government, and nongovernment by convincing them about their business schemes and initiatives.

It has been noticed that both Early Stage and Growth Stage Enterprises face the requirement of medium to long-term finance. The loans provided by Banks and Financial Institutions are repayable in 5–7 years which prevent such enterprises to invest in heavy infrastructure and equipment. Considering that the businesses inherently require some initial investment in the corpus for the long term, equity dilution should not be avoided, though collective enterprises or integrated approach discussed above is always highly recommended as it is a systematic solution to bring them together so that they make more profits as a whole rather than individually.

5.16 CO-CREATION CAN BE WAY FORWARD

In Microfinance, "Self Help Groups" have proved to be a very successful model for collective credit. On the same lines, co-creation can be the next blockbuster. When small entrepreneurs would start putting their resources together, they can enjoy the benefits of scale, such as better negotiation, better access to funds, skill, and technology. They can create business enterprises with better efficiencies in production and ensure a better share of returns. This has proved to be a very successful model in the case of AMUL and can prove to be a systematic solution that improves each aspect of the enterprise. There have also been many cooperatives that have got mired in politics or which stagnated as an organization as members could not have financial or emotional ownership of the institution.

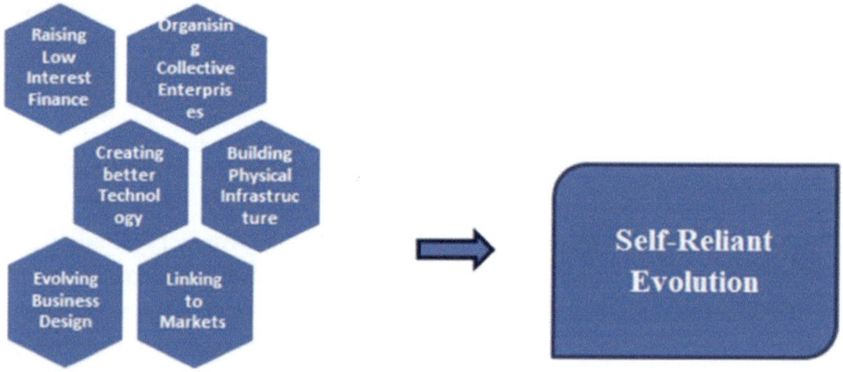

FIGURE 5.1 Self-reliant evolution.

There is an urgent need to learn from previous mistakes and restore lost confidence. Through communication of success stories, field visits, and getting people to see the larger opportunity in creating an enterprise, the extinct model can be transformed into ownership led democratic structure with participatory decision-making. The need is to identify and develop local leadership that sustains and grows the business enterprise while meeting social objectives.

5.17 COMMITMENTS FROM CORPORATE

Fintech Startups have started creating sustainable, surplus generating business enterprises. It would be big support if a large corporate look at them as an opportunity and share the resources and returns. They need to shift their attention toward the startups as not only as investors but also buyers of their products and services. The startups should play a crucial role in the economy as producers, workers, and consumers.

What Fintech Startups require from the large corporate is purchase commitments, technology transfer, and sharing of knowledge and skills. Fintech Startups represent a huge market. They are the people who are interested in producing, buying, and consuming innovative products. If private companies make the effort to cater to this segment, they can tap into a whole new market in the need for quality, healthy and affordable products, and services. This co-evolution of startups and large corporations will help society grow into an empowered and self-reliant structure. Businesses targeting startups can gain from their innovative technology and knowledge on customer segment preferences. For the startups, business from large corporate can increase incomes not only through new economic opportunities but also through increased productivity due to capacity building among employees and business owners and increased access to business inputs.

To conclude, it can be said that technology innovation is not a holistic model. It can provide a solution to the financial sector and empowers them. However, business development involves various nontechnical aspects also. It requires broad-based engagement with all stakeholders to enhance the business and its income-generating capabilities in a structured manner. Undoubtedly, Fintech startups need various kinds of support, such as training, market linkage, hand-holding, mentoring, counseling, etc. It is important to understand the key challenges and strengths of their business and to identify the new entrepreneurship models that would bring about sustainability in Fintech enterprises.

The Incubator and Accelerator model has given a big hope toward bridging the gaps. It has brought a revolutionary change in the status, confidence, and position of entrepreneurs, yet despite being a very good support system, its role in bringing sustainable business development is yet to be seen. The government has also taken several initiatives along with the banks and financial institutions under various schemes, such as Startup India/Stand-Up India, Make in India, and Mudra Schemes to support the growth of startups. Each one of them has contributed in its way in changing the thought process and improving entrepreneurship. However, catering to the Fintech Startups requires all relevant actors to come together and develop a sustainable business model underpinned by innovations which creates a win-all situation for the promoters, investors, and wider stakeholders, such as society, employees, and customers.

The difficulties facing Fintech startups are multifaceted, broadening, and getting more difficult. While traditional business strategies have generally failed and will continue to fail, they have experienced occasional success. Change is made much more challenging by the strong traditional emphasis in the governance, resource management, and risk mitigation frames. This chapter has emphasized strategies that demand little in the way of financial resources, allow for quick outcomes, and offer a number of new institutional and business-led innovations that Fintech Startups may seek to expand upon. The results of the research can result in large increases in employment, the closure of institutional knowledge gaps, and the efficient and effective scaling up of innovation to satisfy the needs of inclusion, sustainability, and growth, ultimately resulting in sustainable Fintech Enterprise.

5.18 CONCLUSION

India, one known as "Soneki Chidiya" has now become dependent on other countries. Talking about the 20th century, in 1978, China's per capita per annum income was around Rs. 1795, whereas of India, it was Rs. 1640 with a difference of just Rs. 155, whereas after 30 years, China's per capita per annum income is around Rs. 565,600, whereas of India, it is around Rs. 165,600. Now the question arises is in the last few years, why this difference grew huge? How China does become the second-largest economy? Well, the answer is simple, China became self-dependent. The same thing is wanted by our honorable Prime Minister, he is dreaming of self-dependent India. He wanted the post-COVID economy to grow in favor of India. This is the reason he has issued the grant of Rs. 20 lakh crore which is 10% of our GDP to be invested for the above purpose. He is encouraging the startups under Make in India and so on. So, the future lies in Fintech companies. Soon, we will see Fintech companies active in every sector. More and more financial giants are interested in this budding industry. In this chapter, we have tried to see the challenges which these companies can face and some strategies which can be adopted to overcome the difficulties. Youth is being encouraged to become entrepreneurs and start investing in these Fintech companies. In the future, the country will be able to curb the traditional problems of corruption or black money and come up with a transparent financial system.

KEYWORDS

- **financial sector**
- **funds**
- **incubator sector**
- **skills**
- **startups**
- **venture capital**
- **emotional intelligence**
- **machine learning**

REFERENCES

Audretsch, D. B. *Innovation and Industry Evolution*; MIT Press, 1995.

Avital, M.; Beck, R.; Beck, R. Beyond Bitcoin: The Rise of Blockchain World. *Computer* **2018,** *51*, 54–58.

Colombelli, A.; Krafft, J.; Vivarelli, M. To Be Born Is Not Enough: The Key Role of Innovative Startups. *Small Busi. Econ.* **2016,** *47* (2), 277–291.

The FinTech Revolution: A Wave of Startups Is Changing finance for the better. *Economist* **2015,** *415* (8937), 13.

Fitzsimmons, J. A.; Fitzsimmons, M. J. *Service Management: Operations, Strategy, Information Technology*, 6th ed.; McGraw-Hill/Irwin: Boston, 2008.

Friedlmaier, M., Tumasjan, A.; Welpe, I. M. Disrupting Industries with Blockchain: The Industry, Venture Capital Funding, and Regional Distribution of Blockchain Ventures. In *51st Hawaii International Conference on System Sciences*; Waikoloa Village, 2018; pp 3517–3526.

Froehle, C. M.; Roth, A. V. New Measurement Scales for Evaluating Perceptions of the Technology-Mediated Customer Service Experience. *J. Oper. Manage.* **2004,** *22* (1), 1–21.

Gazel, M.; Schwienbacher, A. Entrepreneurial Fintech Clusters. *Small Busi. Econ* **2020,** 1–21.

Gimpel, H.; Rau, D.; Röglinger, M. Understanding FinTech Startups–a Taxonomy of Consumer-Oriented Service Offerings. *Electron. Markets* **2018,** *28* (3), 245–264.

Guile, B. R.; Quinn, J. B. *Technology in Services: Policies for Growth, Trade, and Employment*; National Academies Press: Washington, DC, 1988.

Guo, Y.; Liang, C. Blockchain Application and Outlook in the Banking Industry. *Financ. Innov.* **2016,** *2*, 24.

Hileman, G.; Rauchs, M. *Global Blockchain Benchmarking Study*; Social Science Research Network; Rochester, NY, 2017.

Kaur, J.; Dogra, M. FinTech Companies in India: A Study of Growth Analysis. *Abhigyan* **2019,** *37* (1), 21–32.

Khiewngamdee, C.; Yan, H. D. The Role of Fintech e-Payment on APEC Economic Development. *J. Phys. Conf. Ser.* **2019,** *1324* (1), 012099).

King, J.; Rossi, M.; Teigland, R. Jumping on the Blockchain Bandwagon: Lessons of the Past and Outlook to the Future. In *37th International Conference on Information Systems*; Dublin, 2016; pp 1–6.

Lee, I.; Shin, Y. J. Fintech: Ecosystem, Business Models, Investment Decisions, and Challenges. *Busi. Horiz.* **2018,** *61* (1), 35–46.

PwC. Blurred Lines: How FinTech Is Shaping financial Services, 2016 March.

Sharifi, O.; Hossein, B. K. Understanding the Financing Challenges Faced by Startups in India. *Int. J. Sci. Technol. Manage.* **2015,** *4* (1), 264–272.

Vijai, C. Fintech in India–Opportunities and Challenges. *SAARJ J. Bank. Insurance Res. (SJBIR)* **2019,** *8*.

Welsch, G.; Dürr, A.; Thiesse, F. A Consolidated Business Model Canvas of Blockchain-Based FinTech Startups: Evidence from Initial Coin Offerings. In *Conference: 15th International Conference on Wirtschaftsinformatik*, 2019 Dec.

Zetzsche, D. A.; Buckley, R. P.; Arner, D. W.; Föhr, L. The ICO Gold Rush: It's a Scam, It's a Bubble, It's a Super Challenge for Regulators. University of Luxembourg Law Working Paper, 2017; pp 17–83.

WEB LINKS

- https://invest-india-revamp-static-files.s3.ap-south-1.amazonaws.com/s3fs-public/Indias%20Fintech%20Landscape_0.pdf
- https://blog.ipleaders.in/fintech-in-india/
- https://www.pwc.in/consulting/financial-services/fintech.html
- https://assets.kpmg/content/dam/kpmg/pdf/2016/06/FinTech-new.pdf
- https://timesnext.com/10-most-successful-fintech-startups-companies-in-india/
- https://www.investindia.gov.in/sector/bfsi-fintech-financial-services
- https://mediciinnercircle.com/wp-content/uploads/2019/03/FintegrateReport_ExecutiveSummary_Final.pdf
- https://www.indembassybern.gov.in/docs/Fintech-Report-2016.pdf
- http://cryptochainuni.com/wp-content/uploads/McKinsey-Company-FinTech-Challenges-and-Opportunities.pdf
- https://www.forbes.com/sites/allbusiness/2019/10/12/fintech-startup-companies-key-challenges/#589862903e45
- https://tracxn.com/explore/Blockchain-Startups-in-India
- (https://www.digitalauthority.me/resources/fintech-marketing-strategies/).

- https://www2.deloitte.com/content/dam/Deloitte/in/Documents/financial-services/in-fs-fintech-india-ready-for-breakout-noexp.pdf
- https://mediciinnercircle.com/wpcontent/uploads/2019/03/FintegrateReport_ExecutiveSummary_Final.pdf
- http://nifm.ac.in/sites/default/files/E-Compendium.pdf
- https://www.mckinsey.com/~/media/mckinsey/industries/financial%20services/our%20insights/bracing%20for%20seven%20critical%20changes%20as%20fintech%20matures/fintechnicolor-the-new-picture-in-finance.ashx
- https://www.forbes.com/sites/allbusiness/2019/10/12/fintech-startup-companies-key-challenges/#59be72113e45
- https://www.pwc.de/de/newsletter/finanzdienstleistung/assets/insurance-inside-ausgabe-4-maerz-2016.pdf
- https://dea.gov.in/sites/default/files/Report%20of%20the%20Steering%20Committee%20on%20Fintech_1.pdf

CHAPTER 6

FinTech: the Financial Sector's Digital Reformation

VIJAY PRAKASH GUPTA[1] and AMIT KUMAR ARORA[2]

[1]*Institute of Business Management, GLA University, Mathura, India*

[2]*KIET Group of Institutions, Delhi-NCR, Ghaziabad, India*

ABSTRACT

Nowadays financial technologies have attracted the global attraction in the financial sector. FinTech has attracted the customers as it is very convenient, transparent, user-friendly and reliable as it has reduced the pen paper work by using digitalization. With the assistance of FinTech technologies within the financial sector, the service providers are which in turn reduce cost and time which helps to increase the efficiency. FinTech includes artificial intelligence (AI), cryptocurrency, augmented reality (AR), and blockchain technology, etc. In the past few years, the use of technology in finance has rapidly increased. So, we must be aware about the changes in financial technologies because finance is one of the important elements for individuals, businessman, and government. Globally, 96% of the consumers are aware about the one of the financial technologies as per the Global FinTech Adoption index 2019 and Indians are on the second position to adopt the same. Demonetization in India also plays a crucial role for the adoption of FinTech in India. As during the Demonetization phase, people were not having any alternative to use the digital technology for finance which boosts the adoption rate in India.

Revolutionary Challenges and Opportunities of Fintech. Shweta Anand, PhD, Shalini Srivastav, PhD, Vikas Garg, PhD, & Geetika Garg (Eds.)

Therefore, this chapter tried to explore the role of FinTech—as a digital change in the financial industry and its revised phases in the banking industry in India. In particular, the study is based on secondary data and it analyzes the systemic transition phases of FinTech-based innovations in the financial and banking system in India. The main area of this chapter is to ascertain the innovation models and development in financial sectors in India. This chapter is additionally trying to seek out the new changes and development in FinTech in the financial sector, which might be used as an innovative tool to trace the progress and pattern of technological development within the banking sector. This research also focused on the most recent financial innovation of FinTech in India.

6.1 INTRODUCTION

FinTech is the short sort of financial technology which means a financial sector encompassing technology in their services. It means an enterprise that gives financial services with the assistance of innovative technologies and software as well as also includes digitalization, smart sensors, artificial intelligence, and block chain technology, etc. that forced financial companies to become tech-savvy by upgrading their traditional practices with the latest technology. Hence, banks have launched digital interfaces through which customers get various banking services just on click. "FinTech" is a term that has now been initiated to elucidate the transition phase of the financial sector, that is, traditional financial services to digital financial services, and from digital to technological, financial services. FinTech uses advanced technology, mainly internet-based technologies to supply financial services in the financial sector. Financial technology has come out as a replacement industry in India, that is, an industry comprising companies that take technical support for various financial services, such as banking, insurance, asset management, and payment. Companies using FinTech as a replacement technology within the finance sector to deliver the financial products that completely satisfy the present customers' expectations.

In India, as per the EY FinTech Adoption Index, out of 100 people, 85 are ready to adopt the Financial Technology, and India is ranking second in adopting the Financial Technologies with the adoption ratio of 85% (FinTech).

6.1.1 *BRIEF HISTORY OF FINTECH*

The term "fintech" was first utilized within the year 2011. FinTech is nowadays considered as a relatively replacement term in the financial business. Gradually, it has grown into a large FinTech industry that is providing financial and banking services across the world. In the early 1900s, businesses have attempted to adopt the dynamic business environment and introduced modern methods of delivering financial services. Nonetheless, in the previous few decades, it seems that the financial sector is quite evidently significant within the evolution of FinTech and therefore the invention of assorted new techniques of delivering financial services across the world.

The 1950s plastic money was launched and further ATMs were introduced which changed the way money was withdrawn from banks. However, due to the introduction of the web within the 1990s, the FinTech industry came into existence and quickly changed the pattern of services delivery with the assistance of monetary technologies and introduced the assorted new services, such as e-payment, that is, NEFT and RTGS, Online shopping, m-banking, mobile wallets, and digitization of banks, etc. The world's first ATM was introduced in year 1967, and PayPal was founded in 1998 and it was the first online payment platform. Furthermore, in 2009, cryptocurrency, Bit coin was launched after Google launched its Google Pay in 2011 which is considered as the transition phase of financial technologies. With the exception of these are numerous other innovations in financial technology laying the trail of FinTech revolution within the financial sector in India as well as in another part of the world.

Initially, the overall public sector banks were not ready to upgrade their traditional banking process. On the other hand, the private sector banks understand the wants of their customers also as learned and accepted what the fashionable world needed and came up with revolutionary changes in their banking services, and thus attracted an outsized customer base. Online banking was first introduced in India within the year 1996.

Nowadays, financial technology has now totally reshaped the face of financial sector, and models of service delivery. The new financial technology continues to grow and encourages investors across the globe, which strongly supports the FinTech industry. Among the various products and services of the financial sector, such as online banking transactions, fund transfer, medical and health insurance, trading of shares, commercial banking, investment and portfolio management are impacted the foremost by the emergence of FinTech.

6.1.2 RESEARCH METHODOLOGY

This research uses an exploratory method to investigate the changes in financial technologies or digital revolutions well phases of technological transitions within the financial sector. This research tries to trace the progress and pattern of technological changes in the financial sector. The study also explains FinTech-based innovations to understand a much better understanding concerning the pattern of technology diffusion. This research is focused on secondary data.

6.1.3 PROBLEM STATEMENT

Financial technologies are making unexpected surge due to growing online payment transactions offerings. This study determines the role of FinTech and its transition phases as well as also explains about the services which are offered by financial service providers, and it gives a detailed description of FinTech because after the demonetization in India, the usage of FinTech has too much increased.

6.1.4 TOP FINTECH COMPANIES IN INDIA

In India, in the last five years, FinTech has seen rapid growth and is expected to grow to 2.4 billion dollars at the end of 2020. FinTech has flourished into a strong sector with a focused growth ahead because the adoption rate of monetary technology in India is so big in comparison to other countries having a 33% adoption rate. It has become a new segment for new businesses. Many FinTech businesses have a different mode of payment. Here are a number of the foremost successful FinTech start-ups in our country.

6.1.4.1 PAYTM

It had been founded in the year 2010 and it is one of the leading digital wallet companies in India. Its mobile wallet is used by numerous Indian consumers. Paytm also makes a specialty of online shopping.

6.1.4.2 PHONEPE

It is a mobile payment app which has been founded in 2015, where the users instantly transfer money and make payments. It had been acquired by Flipkart in 2016 and it has more than 1000 employees.

6.1.4.3 MOBIKWIK

It had been founded in the year 2009 and it is a mobile payments company connecting consumers with merchants and online sellers. There are more than 550 employees in MobiKwik.

6.1.4.4 LENDING KART

It has been started in 2014 and the prime role of the lending kart is to provide business and loans to various enterprises.

6.1.4.5 POLICYBAZAAR

It came into the existence in the year 2008. Policybazaar works as online life insurance and general insurance aggregator. The company is having more than 2,500 employees.

6.1.4.6 BILL DESK

It had been founded in 2000 and it is an online payment system which is utilized by many Indian business organizations and service providers that aids clients in managing, organizing, and paying their continuing and recurring expenses. With the use of a bill desk, customers can receive, review, and pay all of the invoices they get from various suppliers in one location. It gives billers and banks the chance to save processing costs while improving bill presentation, giving customers access to online payment choices, and enhancing customer service. Some Major FinTech Services in Financial Sector in India

FinTech has enlarged the scope of monetary services through digital platforms. Let us have a glance at the first service providers of FinTech:

6.1.5 PEER-TO-PEER LENDING

Financial service providers use a variety of data sources and different credit models to provide clients with quicker and easier access to financing. Peer-to-peer lending offers online services that match together the right borrowers and lenders.

6.1.6 PAYMENT OPTIONS

FinTech Companies has simplified the method of money flow. FinTech has done away with the need for merchant accounts by creating a web portal that makes it simple to accept online and mobile payments. Similar to Paytm and Oxygen Wallet, it facilitates direct payments to checking accounts and safeguards against fraud by tying it to the payee.

6.1.6.1 INVESTMENT IN RETAIL

FinTech companies also provide customized financial services and knowledge to their existing and prospects customers. They help in professional management of money and investment done by the investors as per the precise requirement of individuals, such as Policybazaar, FundsIndia.com, Scrip box, and Bank Bazaar.

6.1.6.2 FUNDING OF EQUITY

Equity funding is the crowd funding platforms that allow entrepreneurs to get funds for his or her new start-ups. It gives a choice to raise funds from an outsized amount of individuals. Such internet providers' platforms are gaining worldwide popularity as public prefers secure finance to challenging venture capital. The users of these services are majorly starting it at a very initial stage of their business.

6.1.6.3 CRYPTOCURRENCY

India still embraces the conservative ways of transaction where cash still overrules. The use of cryptocurrency like "bitcoin" has not gained much popularity within the local markets as compared with the other foreign exchanges. Besides, there are a few of bitcoin exchange started in India, such as Coinsecure, Zebopay, and Unocoin.

6.1.6.4 OTHER INNOVATIVE SOFTWARE

Some financial sectors are experimenting with special features of software, such as artificial intelligence, blockchain to reinforce the accessibility to financial products. Hence, increasing the efficiency in everyday business operations.

FinTech scope is wider at both macro and micro levels. Presently, it renders an array of services, such as software for online trading, accounting, and crafting unique technological platforms to attach buyers and sellers in specific industries.

6.1.7 FINANCIAL TECHNOLOGY TRENDS AND FUTURE OF INDIAN BANKING

The digital transformations within the banking sector in India show how banking service provider interacts and doing daily business transactions, apart from this, innovation and advancements will make changes in working of financial system and it influences the future of banking, that is, retail, mobile, online, and digital banking technology in India. Increasing demand for digital banking has changed the face of the banking system in India and experiencing transformation within the entire banking system operations. Below are some major emerging technological trends in banking and financial services that are mentioned and explained.

6.1.8 ARTIFICIAL INTELLIGENCE (AI)

AI is taken into account as an emerging technology trend and way forward for Indian banking sector, and nowadays, it is mainly used by all financial and banking institutions for the streamline customer experiences with the assistance of robots and chatbots. AI is also used by the banking sector for its mobile banking customers to facilitate access for any banking operations. It also helps financial institutions to work along with other trends, such as big data analytics, voice interfaces, and RPA because it is also believed that AI is giving business advantage for the financial sector through cost savings, security and forestall, and detect fraud and is efficient in working by delivering better services to its customers with full satisfaction.

6.1.9 CLOUD COMPUTING

Nowadays cloud computing is one of the better option and superior technology for the financial system, and it helps to boost the efficiency, accessibility, and capacity to store and save data of its customers with proper security. With the assistance of cloud computing, banks can easily access the centrally stored data whenever they require. Accessing the cloud can increase banks' ability to innovate "by enhancing agility, efficiency, and productivity." Aside from this, Cloud adaptation also creates a multi-channel relationship with their customer which helps banks in maintaining and improving their customer service.

6.1.10 CLOUD BANKING

Cloud banking is additionally considered as one of the future technologies and might be a mechanism for banking and financial sectors. Cloud banking system has emerged as game changer for financial services. Organizations will operate in the near future because cloud banking is often easily integrated with another ecosystem or FinTech company in pace. Banking and financial sectors mainly adopting cloud banking because of the actual fact that banks want to reduce their costs of operation and better may offer for product and service across the retail and corporate banking segments. Moreover, banks can decide the storage of knowledge in public cloud, private cloud, or hybrid cloud as per the business decision. Cloud banking also can help financial institutions to fulfill the regulatory and compliance framework levied by the RBI or other regulatory authorities.

6.1.11 BUSINESS PROCESS AS A SERVICE (B-PAAS)

The emerging trend in coming days in Bank and Financial Institutions is that these institutions would really like to leverage financial technology and pay just for services offered by the product/software vendors by which banks will gain various benefits with B-Paas like

- They are going to be ready to pay the cost of the software license.
- They also will be ready to reduce the value of operation and maintenance of the data center.
- The payment for service offered by the software vendors is going to be supported by the transaction volume or user-based licenses.
- Banks often easily move to any geographical location with pre-configured products.

6.1.12 CYBER SECURITY

Money and Banking is taken into account together. This industry deals with sensitive and personal information of their customers, and it has become an attractive target for cybercriminals. Though it is most vital also as essential for service providers to supply security of cash and privacy and of their customers, thanks to which, nowadays, financial institutions are adopting the safety measures and prepared with the plans to attenuate the damage if any mishap occurs. Banks must share best practices and knowledge to assist customers avoid the probabilities of cyberattacks.

6.1.13 ROBOTIC PROCESS AUTOMATION (RPA)

Using the robotic process automation system, the bank can use it for general and basic customer service, such as account balance check, transaction queries, request for cheque, and demand draft to save lots of the time and energy of bank personals and customers both. Besides improving productivity, this also helps to reduce operational costs and therefore the error rate. With instant resolution through RPA, users can make a fast decision for his or her MasterCard application without getting any human agents involved within the process.

6.1.14 CHALLENGES OF FINANCIAL TECHNOLOGY

In recent times, innovations in financial technology have been revolutionized that how we interact with our finances has significantly changed how we handle money. While some businesses are leading those changes, there are still numerous obstacles to overcome this year before an industry can be completely disrupted. These are the main issues that FinTech in many industries, particularly banking and finance, must address as soon as possible.

6.1.15 CYBERCRIME IN FINANCIAL SECTOR

With the use of ICT and the internet in the banking sector, risk of cybercrimes has increased day by day. Although banks are doing their best to keep the record of customers safe and maintaining the privacy policy for safety and security of their account, it sometimes it becomes very difficult to main the privacy and protect customers as well as company information and other information from cybercrime risk. To fight with this cybercrime problems, there are so many solutions that are developed to protect the data and information that are followed by FinTech industries. Blockchain mechanism is considered one of the important solutions and tools to control these issues.

6.1.16 USES OF THE BIG DATA USE IN FINANCIAL SERVICES

The Big Database is one of the opportunities for banking services as well as it is an obstacle for FinTech service providers. With the help of customer databases, the banks and financial service providers can trace the record of their customers to provide them a better service. But the bigger and unstructured data can be the starting place of the higher risk. So, to overcome these problems, there is a need for powerful data analytics technology for the benefits and protection of Big Data. Moreover, nowadays too many data analytics solutions are up-and-coming with controllable transaction risks.

6.1.17 FINTECH DISRUPTION OF FINANCIAL INDUSTRY

Economic situation and business are too much dynamic, due to which the small FinTech companies are unable to grow with a changing environment and unable to adopt the changes in the economic cycle and suffering losses. One of the main reasons for the disorder of the Financial Industry is an irregular distribution of FinTech technologies due to which financial houses are unable to calculate the growth potential of their companies.

6.1.18 CREDIBILITY/TRUST COMPONENT

The major challenges of any technological transformation and innovation are credibility, and it holds good for FinTech too. As we are aware that in monetary people, still lack the trust component. To gain the confidence of people, for FinTech, it takes a lot of time and efforts.

6.1.19 CUSTOMER EXPERIENCE IN THE FINANCIAL SERVICE

Customer experience, expectations, and satisfaction are the most important issues for the various industries and firms, especially in the service Industry or financial services provider. In current business and economics scenario, customers are more focused on hard cash, because cash in hand in physical form gives much satisfaction as compared with plastic money or money in digital form. Due to the more focus on physical importance of money or cash in hand, customers are not understanding the utility and importance of e-banking, m-banking, or other financial instruments, and they do not care whether the bank is FinTech or not.

6.1.20 REGULATORY COMPLIANCE IN FINANCE

Compliance as a general term means acting according to a set of rules or regulations, the regulatory environment is one of the important components of the business environment and its changes from time to time as the need and economic situations. So, the ever-changing regulatory compliance by the regulatory bodies is the challenges for the financial institutions. Regulatory compliance protects consumers and investors, and it ensures efficient, transparent, and fair markets which reduces crime within financial services and maintains the confidence of consumers in the wider financial system.

6.1.21 FINTECH REVOLUTION IN INDIA

Nowadays, the approach to life of the people has become much easier and fast like for commuting from one place to a different place, we are taking services of Ola and Uber, ordering foods from Swiggy or Food Panda, and the words "Paytm Karo" and "Phone Pay" have been engrained within the consumer's mind. Digital transformation and innovations have touched our lives subtly in numerous ways. The foremost important development is that the emergence of FinTech firms. They hold the potential to cause a paradigm shift in the way financial services are delivered. India has also experienced the marvel of monetary technology within the financial and banking sector. Now, India is transforming toward cash-driven economy to a cashless society.

Due to beginning of digital innovation and implementation of financial technologies in financial sector, it has changed the way people do their daily financial transactions and handling of their money. It has been observed that within the past few years, FinTech has become one among the foremost buzzing sectors in India.

Additionally, indigenous firms playing a really crucial role within the development of the financial sectors by offering various services, such as e-banking, mobile wallet, e-purse, and many more.

According to a report "Future of Consumption in Fast-Growth Consumer Markets: India by the world Economic Forum and Bain & Company," The consumption level of internet data in India will increase four-fold by 2030 with over 1 billion active internet users especially young generation (Ojha and Ingilizian, 2019). The Indian populace has been very receptive to the trend of digitization as evident by the Smartphone explosion, increasing digital payments, expanding e-commerce market, rising consumption of digital entertainment and use of food delivery apps and particularly online banking and financial transactions.

This presents a perfect scenario for the expansion of FinTech firms in India. There are over 900 FinTech firms in India. Digital lending which includes capital financing, peer-to-peer lending and SME lending constitutes 31% of the FinTech industry followed by digital payments at 25% (NASSCOM and Zinnov, 2018). Many global firms, such as Google Pay, Amazon Pay have also entered the Indian FinTech landscape.

6.2 USES AND RELEVANCE OF FINTECH

The below-mentioned examples show how and where the FinTech is being used.

Image credit: Prakash Donga

6.2.1 BLOCKCHAIN AND CRYPTOCURRENCY

Block chain is the newest form of technology especially adopted in the financial sector nowadays. It is based on a peer-to-peer (P2P) topology, by allowing digital information to be distributed but not copied and that keeps track of a digital asset's provenance. In the real world, block chain first appeared in 2016 and 2017. Because of transactions and data sharing between open and private corporate networks, block chain technology is more efficient in the banking and financial services industries.

6.2.2 EXCHANGE, STOCK

Trading Apps , Robo advising, and Robo advisors are among the financial digital platforms that can easily do the automated, algorithm-based financial planning services with very less intervention of human supervision. With the help of the FinTech, investors can do the trading with less risk and more efficiently and easy ways. New technology and innovation in financial sector and stock exchange also attracted investor for more participation in trading and investment.

6.2.3 RESEARCH

Nowadays FinTech is employed in marketing research to seek out the causes of any incidence that happened in the economic environment. By using the FinTech, the experts of share market and financial sector are feeling very happy to explore the most reasons of the fluctuations in their business and stock prices. With the assistance of FinTech research, business home is ready to do the SWOT analysis of their business and ready to take the acceptable action and counter measures against the threats of the business.

6.2.4 DIGITAL MONEY

Digital currency is a type of virtual currency available in electronic form. It has just like properties similar to physical currencies, but it can be used for cross-border and immediate as well as transfer of ownership. Few examples of digital currencies are cryptocurrencies, and digital currency issued by the apex bank.

The digital money and FinTech have already radically altered the landscape of the economic system in the world. Thanks to digitalization and innovations in the financial sector, it changes the face of monetary institutions both customers and financial service providers are mutually benefited by the benefits of monetary technology.

6.2.5 ONLINE BANKING

A user of online banking can do all financial transactions with the help of the Internet and without visiting a bank and waiting in the queue for a long time for just basic banking work like enquiry of balance or printing of passbook also. Nowadays, most of the traditional banks offer online access to their customers to access their savings and current accounts. Online banking helps users to view their updated balances, fund, and make payments. The younger generations are comfortable with the web banking and mobile banking and that they do the financial transactions on a smartphone on click within a fraction of minutes.

A customer can conveniently use the online banking service from home or office anytime, anywhere.

6.2.6 *INVESTMENT AND BUDGETING APPS*

It is one of the foremost common uses of FinTech lately, that is, investment and budgeting apps for consumers are now very popular since few years and growing exponentially. Investment and Budgeting Apps are being used by users to make their own investment portfolio and budgets, gather checks, or navigate excel spreadsheets to stay track of their finances. It helps individuals trace the record of their daily income, as well as payment received on daily or monthly, expenditures done on a daily and monthly basis and many more things related to individual financial budget on their mobile device.

6.2.7 *SCOPE FOR THE GROWTH IN INDIA*

Indian financial system and financial technology may be younger, but it is developing in very fast speed, financial sectors are expanding their business and services in a marketplace, an innovation and technological development in financial services are acts as a catalyst for the growth opportunities for financial service providers. Apart from this, brightening and supporting government policies are also promoted for the growth of start-ups in FinTech in India. At the same time, both conventional banking institutions and NBFCs are also playing vital role in its growth. The report of NASSCOM pronounced that around 400 FinTech companies are operated in India, which will boost the financial sector and offer the product to their customers in technological upgrade form.

It is expected and projected by NASSCOM that India's FinTech software market may increase across US$ 2.4 billion by 2020, which may be double of the present rate of growth.

The companies who are offering FinTech services are currently redefining the way for service providers. Since few years, it has been observed that FinTech companies are increasing very rapidly. In the past few years, the investment in FinTech has increased with high speed which record speed—tripling to US$ 12.2 billion in 2014 from US$ 4.05 billion in 2013, and reaching US$ 19.1 billion in 2015. Additionally, India has a big untapped marketplace for financial service provider and financial technology start-ups because approximately, 25% of the 74 population are still do not have bank account as well as approximately, 70% of payments are made in cash.

In India, it has been observed and anticipated both mobile and internet users will be on top in the world and expected to boom in 80–90 percentage in 2020 from 65–75% currently, which will be the major factor for the growth ability of FinTech in India.

As per the Earth FinTech Report 2018, "The majority of profitable FinTech companies have struggled to develop on their own because they have concentrated on certain tasks, markets, or operations that have high degrees of friction or that are underserved by conventional financial institutions. Traditional financial institutions are well-funded and have a large customer base, but outdated technologies are holding them back.

6.2.8 FUTURE OF FINTECH IN INDIA

Very soon, India is going to become one in all the leading nations in FinTech innovation. The government of India has done the fabulous job by taking an initiative called the "Jan Dhan Yojana" scheme and it is considered a decent effort of the government to popularize cashless transactions.

In India, the financial sector, FinTech is one of the innovative tools which is being adopted by FinTech firms. As per the survey conducted by EY FinTech Adoption Index 2019, FinTech adaptation in India is extremely high, the adoption rate is 85%, and progressing to becoming a frontrunner in adopting the FinTech, Digital wallets, m-banking, e-banking, and other digital tools and plenty of more modern innovations just like the Unified Payment Interface (UPI) platform and digital technologies and has moved forward to the adoption of FinTech services.

The adoption of FinTech and digital services has increased extensively within the last few years in India. India is in the runner-up in the FinTech adoption rate in the global platform.

The growth of the FinTech services aided by such a big amount of economic and noneconomic such as Indian economy is increasing day by day and becomes the top 5 economy of the world. Apart from this observing good economic process and development, the population of youth, exits of innovative technologies—and so many budding entrepreneurs are emerging with a brand new business start-up, and also, drive of tech-savvy young technocrats have anticipated that the growth of FinTech in India will uplift in forthcoming days. As rightly said by Arora and Panchal (2019), the government of India should motivate the FinTech companies, so that India can be in the first place in the FinTech adoption as we are currently in the second position.

6.3 CONCLUSION

By examining and analyzing the various facts, figures, and data, it has been anticipated that the emergence of FinTech services in India will move with full velocity. It is also the most important proven analysis that India has gigantic technological potential and so many budding entrepreneurs are also in the race. It has been found that more than 1000 plus FinTech start-up has emerged and are operating in India. IoT and Blockchain are the most important tools which are being used nowadays in financial sector, that is why both technically and financially, the FinTech firms should adopt and acknowledge it at faster rate. It has been observed that majority of the financial service providers have successfully adopted the FinTech and it is expected an equivalent with the other financial segments as well. The FinTech industry must be more supported and promoted by government and other regulatory bodies with different schemes and initiatives. So, digitalization and other innovative technologies in conjunction with ICT are changing the scenario of commercial sector especially the financial services and it is expected to be one among the biggest gainers. The rise of FinTech is a very important indicator of the growth and expansion of financial services.

KEYWORDS

- **FinTech**
- **digitalization and innovation**
- **artificial intelligence**
- **blockchain**
- **ICT**

REFERENCES

Arner, D. W.; Barberis, J.; Buckley, R. P. The Evolution of Fintech: A New Post-Crisis Paradigm. *Geo. J. Int. L.* **2015,** *47*, 1271.

Arora, A. K.; Panchal, A. FinTech: New Financial Landscape in India. *Manag. Account. J.* **2019,** *54* (10), 26–29.

Dubey, V. FinTech Innovations in Digital Banking. *Int. J. Eng. Res. Technol.* **2019,** *8* (10), 2278–0181.

Gupta, V. P.; Agarwal, P. K. Comparative Study of Customer Satisfaction in Public Sector and Private Sector Banks in India (A Case Study of Meerut Region of UP). *Int. J. Manag. MIT College Manag.* **2013,** *1* (1), 56–63.

Gupta, V. P.; Agarwal, P. K. Comparative Study of Customer Satisfaction in Public and Private Sector Banks in India (A Case Study Of Meerut Region of U. P.). *Glob. J. Bus. Manag.* **2013,** *7* (1).

Gupta, V. P.; Arora, A. K. Automation in Healthcare Services. In *Applications of Deep Learning and Big IoT on Personalized Healthcare Services*; IGI Global, 2020; pp. 1–19.

Gupta V. P.; Agarwal P. K.; Tyagi A. K. A Descriptive Study of Service Quality & Customer Satisfaction with Special Reference to the Commercial Banking Industry in India. *NIET J. Manag.* **2013–2014**(Winter)**,** *6* (2), 43–54, ISSN No. 09757643.

Gupta, V. P.; Bansal, D. Theoretical and Empirical Development in Management and IT; 2018, pp. 64–73.

https://blog.iese.edu/xvives/files/2018/02/EE_2.2017.pdf#page=99 googleshcolars

https://tearsheet.co/new-banks/banking-2020-technology-trends-and-the-future-of-banking/

https://towardsdatascience.com/emerging-technology-trends-for-banking-industry-in-2020-beyond-b6ec30f2c102

https://www.accenture.com/in-en/insight-future-fintech-banking

https://www.easyleadz.com/blog/fintech-companies-in-india/

https://www.enterpriseedges.com/fintech-ecosystem-in-india

https://www.forbes.com/sites/bernardmarr/2019/11/08/the-7-biggest-technology-trends-to-disrupt-banking--financial-services-in-2020/#3e027a322c42

https://www.investindia.gov.in/sector/bfsi-fintech-financial-services

https://www.mindtree.com/blog/emerging-technology-trends-shaping-future-banking-financial-services

https://www.toptal.com/finance/investment-banking-freelancer/fintech-and-banks

Lagarde, C. Central Banking and Fintech: A Brave New World. *Innov. Technol. Gov. Glob.* **2018,** *12* (1–2), 4–8.

Van Loo, R. Making Innovation More Competitive: The Case of Fintech. *UCLA L. Rev.* **2018,** *65*, 232.

Vasiljeva, T.; Lukanova, K. Commercial Banks and FINTECH Companies in the Digital Transformation: Challenges for the Future. *J. Bus. Manag.* **2016,** *11*, 45–34.

CHAPTER 7

Global Understanding of Fintech

AMANJOT KAUR[1] and HARPREET SINGH[2]

[1]*Bhai Gurdas Institute of Management and Technology, Sangrur, Punjab, India*

[2]*Punjab Institute of Management and Technology, Alour, Khanna, India*

ABSTRACT

Fintech is the new application, procedure, item, or plan of action in the budgetary administration industry, which is made out of at least one integral money-related administrations and presents as a start-to-finish process by means of the Internet. In simple words, Fintech is the blend of the words "budgetary" and "innovation." This is a rising industrial sector that utilizes the latest innovations for the development of exercises in an account. With the discovery of Fintech, the traditional financial methods come to an end. In this chapter, we cover information about Fintech, its uses, challenges, and how it works. This chapter provides a detailed insight into the concept of Fintech, its key components, utility along with some examples of Fintech companies. The major challenges in the world economy which encourage innovation and developments in the Fintech field have also been discussed. Overall, the chapter provides information about the current scenario of Fintech and major challenges faced by the Fintech agencies throughout the world.

Revolutionary Challenges and Opportunities of Fintech. Shweta Anand, PhD, Shalini Srivastav, PhD, Vikas Garg, PhD, & Geetika Garg (Eds.)

7.1 INTRODUCTION

Fintech alludes to the mix of innovation to contribution by budgetary administration organizations so as to improve their utilization and conveyance of purchasing. Fintech fundamentally works by unbundling contributions by such firms and making new markets for them (Investopedia, 2019). Fintech is nowadays rapidly turning into a worldwide wonder that is driven by trendsetters and is followed intently by scholastics while drawing the consideration of controllers. Extensively, Fintech is an umbrella term meant for inventive innovation-empowered monetary administrations and the plan of actions that go with those administrations (Mention, 2019). In other words, it can be described as the following:

The innovations related to money, generally known as Fintech, are the innovations and developments that intend to contend with customary strategies regarding money as the conveyance related to budgetary administration (Lin, 2015). This is a rising industrial sector that utilizes the latest innovations for the development of exercises in an account (Schuffel, 2016). The utilization of smart mobile phones for portable banking services contributing toward administration and digital money are examples of advances in planning toward making monetary administration available to the general public. The budgetary innovation entities consist of the two new organizations which are set up as money-related establishments including innovation organizations that attempt to supplement or improve the utility of monetary administrations already provided by existing monetary organizations (Sanicola, 2017).

7.2 WHAT IS FINANCIAL TECHNOLOGY—FINTECH?

The budgetary-related innovation, that is, Fintech, is used to describe the technology that attempts to develop and robotize the utility and conveyance of money related to administration. In this order, Fintech is used to assist organizations, entrepreneurs, as well as shoppers to deal with their budgetary practices, procedures, and lives by utilizing specific programming and statistics that are performed on personal computers and progressively on mobile phones. Overall, the word "Fintech" is a combination of "money-related innovation."

7.2.1 UNDERSTANDING FINTECH

Comprehensively, as an expression, "monetary innovation" could be applied to any advancement such as how businesses are being executed by individuals, starting from the creation of computerized cash up to twofold sectional accounting. Since the web unrest as well as the portable web and cell phone insurgency, in any of the case, monetary innovations have improved exponentially and Fintech, which initially alluded to personal computer innovations, has been applied to bank's back offices or exchanging firms. Presently, Fintech depicts a wide range of assortment of mechanical mediation into individuals and business accounts. Fintech now also represents an assortment of monetary practices and procedures, including cash moves, storing of data in your mobile or cell phones, bypassing a branch of the bank for raising fund, raising fund for a business start-up or proceedings of your ventures, by and large without the assistance of an individual. As indicated by Fintech Adoption Index 2017, almost one-third of the customers use Fintech services from two or more companies over any rate. Additionally, the minds of shoppers are inhibited by Fintech as a part of their day-to-day lives (Kagan, 2019).

An article, *10 Things Consumers Need to Know about Fintech*, published by Consumers International explained the term as:

Finance + Technology + Fintech = A Revolution in Financial Services (copyright Consumers International, 2020).

The blend of money and innovation is the same old thing. Money-related foundations have a long history of embracing new innovation, for example, ATMs, credit cards, and chip and pin were the new radicals at one time. Nonetheless, Fintech is upsetting the shape and delivery of financial services on a lot bigger scale. From miniaturized scale remittances and shared loan-giving to cell-phone spending organizers and mobile payments, new organizations are bypassing the established monetary middle men and establishments. They are delivering items and services to consumers directly. Given that half of the population in the world is utilizing one Fintech service in any event, you are most likely utilizing one already. What is more, in the event that you live in India or China, it is almost certain with 75% shoppers are already utilizing Fintech products.

7.2.2 DEFINITIONS

Fintech is characterized as products and organizations that utilize the recently created, advanced and online advances in the banking and money-related administration enterprises.

1. The effect that Fintech makes in the economy is still in its infancy. It is pretty much enhancing the way banking, loaning, and capital market work (Raznick).
2. A main Fintech firm is another type of organization that offer credits through online platforms (Martin, 2020).
3. Traditional banks are eager about using Fintech as their clients, accomplices, or merchants—for the most part in all the three jobs without a moment's delay (Calvey).[10]
4. An examination on the meaning of Fintech is presumed to be: "Fintech is another monetary industry that applies innovation to improve money-related exercises" (Schueffel, 2017).
5. Fintech can likewise be considered as "any innovative thoughts that improve budgetary help forms by proposing innovation arrangements as indicated by various business circumstances, while the thoughts could likewise prompt new models of business or even new organizations" (Leong and Sung, 2018).

7.3 EXAMPLES OF FINTECH (SRADERS, 2019)

How Fintech was utilized during 2020 and is it a part of conventional employment?

7.3.1 CROWDFUNDING AGENCIES

Organizations such as Kickstarter, GoFundMe, Patreon, and others show the possible scope of Fintech beyond conventional banking.

Crowdfunding stages permit web as well as applications to deliver or obtain funds from anyone else on the platform, while permitted people and organizations manage financing from an assortment of resources in a common spot.

Instead of going to a conventional bank for a credit, it is now conceivable to go directly to financial specialists for help and the specialists keeping in mind their applications, extend subsidizing to financing. Moreover, the quantity of crowdfunding stages has been increased throughout the year.

7.3.2 BLOCKCHAIN AND CRYPTOCURRENCY

Cryptographic money along with Blockchain is a trademark instance related to Fintech in real life. Cryptographic money trades Coinbase and Gemini engage clients for purchasing and selling digital currencies such as bitcoin and litecoin.

In any case, notwithstanding Crypto and Blockchain administrations, BlockVerify, a blockchain-based system assists in diminishing extortion by keeping provenance information over the Blockchain. Further, keeping in mind that Cryptographic money and Blockchain might be fairly dubious in Fintech industry, they still have held pieces of the venture world by storm as of late.

7.3.3 MOBILE PAYMENTS

Since everybody has a cell phone nowadays, they utilize some type of mobile payments. The global mobile payment market size was estimated at USD 40.59 billion in 2021 and is expected to reach USD 52.21 billion in 2022..

Utilizing progressively refined innovation, administrations have developed applications that permit shoppers to trade cash and payments on the web or on cell phones—including well-known payment applications Venmo, Apple (AAPL), and Alibaba (BABA), who got into the versatile payment business through Apple Pay and Alipay.

7.3.4 INSURANCE

Fintech also disturbed the insurance business by incorporating a range of vehicle protection, home protection, and information assurance services.

7.4 WHICH ARE FINTECH COMPANIES?

A Fintech organization is the one that fabricates the innovation or application for money-related reason. Numerous customary money-related foundations utilize Fintech to improve their procedure and they work with Fintech administrations, or at times, they build up their own application (Quora).

7.5 HOW DOES FINTECH WORKS?

Fintech is definitely not another industry; it is the only one that has developed rapidly. Innovation has somewhat consistently been a piece of the money-related world, regardless of whether it is the presentation of credit cards during the 1950s or ATMs, electronic exchanging floors, individual account applications, and high-recurrence exchanging during the decades that followed. (Copyright builtin 2019.)

The motive behind money-related innovation shifts from undertaking to extend, application to application. The most current advances, in any case, use artificial intelligence (AI) calculations, Blockchain, and information science to do everything from process credit risks to run flexible investments. Indeed, there is presently a whole subset of administrative innovation named "regtech" intended to explore the mind-boggling universe of consistence and administrative issues of ventures like Fintech.

7.5.1 USES

Fintech is disrupting each segment of the money-related industry.

In spite of the fact that this business invokes pictures of new businesses and industry-evolving innovation, customary organizations and banks are likewise continually receiving Fintech administrations for their own motivations. Here is a brief explanation of how the business is both disrupting and improvising on a few territories:

1. Banking
2. Cryptocurrency and Blockchain
3. Machine Learning and Trading
4. Payments

5. Lending
6. Insurance

7.6 MAJOR KEY ISSUES THAT HELP STARTINGA FINTECH COMPANY

Various Fintech new businesses (Harroch and Guzy, 2019) show incredible growth guarantee and are rapidly winning rising business sector valuations. A portion of the same kind of organizations has developed and continues developing for a huge amount of money. New companies, which are establishing their new business in the Fintech world, have to cope up with various problems and difficulties through administration for not only raising money but also for serious issues that we will discuss. Ten of those key issues and difficulties are given in Section 7.6.1.

7.6.1 INCREASING ENTREPRENEURISM, STRATEGIC FINANCING

Increasing entrepreneurism financing is never simple in technological financial organizations. Adventure financial specialists will bring up various key issues including the following:

- Challenges in money-related procedure are the organization's answer hoping to Fintech.
- A certified supervisory crew.
- Market offers should be enormous.
- There should be optimistic footing for the organization accomplishment and right on time or leader clients.
- The originators should be energetic, also decided.
- The originators comprehend the primary monetary and measured their business.
- The originators get alluded by speculators through a confided in associate. (It is incredibly hard to get an endeavor financial specialist intrigued through cold pitching or cold messages.)
- Financial specialist pitch deck proficient and intriguing. (underneath regarding your speculator pitch deck ought to contain.)
- The probable dangers to the business particularly are administrative hazards.

- There are some reasons for the organization's item or administration extraordinary.

Method used for venture capital be utilized and progression involved and sufficient to acquire the following round of financing.

- The normal price about organization practicals.
- The organization has separated innovation.
- The organization's licensed innovation.
- The organization's money-related forecast is practical and fascinating.
- In a perfect world, Fintech organizations will pull in the correct funding speculators with Fintech experience and the privilege of vital financial specialists.

Here are a few instances of professional Fintech speculators who help Fintech organizations:

- Give market, item, and serious insight.
- Provide help which refines the promotion of the scheme and the client aim list.
- Give acquaintances with future clients; probable key accomplices include suppliers of obligation capitalize; funding speculators intrigued by the Fintech space; and potential supervisory crew individuals.

Vital Fintech speculators can be the following:

(1) Pilot clients
(2) Dispersion accomplices
(3) Specialized and item guides
(4) Vital accomplices working together on item improvement
(5) Supportive in giving understanding into administrative issues
(6) Mergers and Acquisitions are search parties of the Fintech organization

Nonetheless, Fintech organizations should abstain from conceding an excessive number of rights (for example, privileges of the first refusal at a bargain for organization), as this would scare or slaughter further raising of money or mergers and acquisition openings. Furthermore, fitting item advancement for the requirements for key speculator transforms a beginning to hostage improvement group.

7.6.2 GREAT CAPITALIST PITCH DECK

The monetary subject matter experts and indispensable examiners intend to work with the conservative and interesting blueprint of the trade as even they are not gathering data and social occasion. Accordingly, it is critical that a Fintech start-up makes an incredible financial specialist pitch deck that recounts to a convincing story and shows adaptability.

The employer needs speculator pitch deck to cover the accompanying subjects, generally as request plan with these following titles:

- Organization Survey (an outline review of the organization).
- Strategic innovation.
- Group (includes key cooperative individuals and their significant foundation).
- Challenges (the huge issues we are attempting to understand).
- Solution (what is your proposed arrangement? For what reason is it superior to different arrangements or items).
- Market Offers (addressable market is enormous).
- Products (points of interest for not only item but also administration).
- Consumers (objective clients and the reasons that force them to choose these kinds of organization).
- Technology (the basic innovation and way of separation).
- Competitors (the primary contenders and the method used to become superior to opposition).
- Footing (early clients, early adopters, incomes, press, and associations).
- Plan of Action (work and income model which is adaptable and the obtaining expenses and tenacity).
- Marketing Plan (intend to showcase and to foresee client procurement prices as compared with the lifetime estimation of the client).
- Economic (forecast incomes, main suspicions, EBITDA). Progress you are attempting to rise and progress will you make with that capital).

Useful pitch deck tips are given below:

- Market offers will be enormous.
- Depict ability in the group.
- Try not to give exorbitant monetary subtleties. Hit the key pointers and spare the rest for development.
- Try not to attempt to wrap all the aspects of the pitch deck. Personal introduction will offer a chance to include and feature key data.
- Utilize English—an excess of language or abbreviations can divert from your story and you will lose believability.
- Try not to think little of or put down the opposition, or excuse the administrative dangers.
- Ensure that your data and measurements are cutting edge.
- "Look and feel" affairs. Consider speculator articulation and get proficient assistance from a visual fashioner.
- Audit and try out decks for thoughts on the introduction.
- Make it certain to incorporate the accompanying base, left of the pitch deck spread page: "Classified and proprietary. Copyright (c) by [Name of Company]. All Rights Reserved."

7.6.3 REGULATORY ISSUES FOR FINTECH COMPANIES

On the off chance that you are in the Fintech space, you ought to envision that managing the guideline will turn into a day-to-day standard. There is expanding pressure on the new Fintech companies, all-inclusive, to give directions to manage existing or future administrative obstacles. The crucial thing is to do tasks by controllers and ensure the contract with colleagues committed to learning the patterns can bond with the suitable administrative form to have strong comprehension of any administrative effect on the item or the manner in which it has a showcase item.

As a start-up, it is essential to know about the administrative structure. The main matter has the following:

Manage organization's items or administrations.

- Old guidelines have organization consent.
- Some legal formalities such as license should be requiring.
- Cooperate with the organization's necessary license.

To accomplish, there may be requirement of financial part from the organization's point of view. A long-haul approach or a middle person step is needed for this.

In the event that the organization is managing protections, stores, and additionally giving out loan, at that point lawful direction ought to be counseled on a suitable methodology before advertising it to the shoppers.

Security and assurance of individual data is an immense issue at this moment, with new laws being formulated throughout the world. Indeed, even big budget organizations are battling to stay up to date of new prerequisites. The accompanying buyer protection, information security-related, and money-related administrations, which have a direct relation with the law or administrative plans, are important for Fintech organizations:

1. Federal Trade Commission.
2. Consumer Financial Protection Bureau.
3. European Union GDPR Rules.
4. Telephone Consumer Protection Act.
5. State data breach notification laws.
6. CAN-SPAM rules.
7. Evolving federal and state laws.
8. Gramm-Leach-Bliley Act.
9. New York Department of Financial Services Cybersecurity Rules.
10. Anti-money laundering laws.
11. International laws.

7.6.4 CONTENDING WITH ENORMOUS COMMERCIAL BRANDS

Nowadays, these organizations, for example, Goldman Sachs, Citi, or PayPal, are not just rivals with enormous existing monetary powerhouses; however long before that, they should fight with Amazon and other innovation organizations venturing into money-related services. A Fintech start-up cannot disparage the spending intensity of the officeholders and their readiness to spend with regards to coordinated shopper advertising. A Fintech organization requires separate items, benefits, and also guarantees faultlessness. The objective market may be inadequately comprehended or underserved, or the customers are essentially disappointed with the present contributions. In the foundation space, it may be another pattern is developing and another arrangement connects an item hole or lessons rubbing.

As "open banking" extends all-inclusive facilities alongside PSD2 (the European Payment Services Directive relevant to the installments business) and GDPR, a new door is opening for Fintech organizations. Presentation of introduced guidelines is making everything fair and opening new doors for products and services in both B2C and B2B spaces.

Albeit huge occupants have attempted to discourse these changes, so most parts are slower than the normal Fintech organization; the speed to advertise is a significant upper hand, yet, is not be reasonable over the long haul.

A Fintech B2C organization ought to have the option to answer the accompanying issues.

- The issue you have to understand that the huge occupants are not tending to, and give reason that they are overlooking that market fragment or opportunity.
- You are attempting to change client conduct. Assuming this is the case, your methodology you will choose and give reason that you think it is conceivable.
- The clients are gambling in the event that they receive your answer versus an occupant's item.
- You will be able to fabricate trust with your clients.
- The capacity that officeholders will respond. Also, on the off chance that they do, to what extent will it take them.
- Any innovation that is faultless with your answer.

For a B2B organization, the inquiries revolve around item separation and the issue you can fathom for the venture. Recollect that the item needs to take care of a critical issue for an enormous organization to wager on a start-up versus a bigger, progressively settled organization. The accompanying rundown features are the most basic that focuses on:

- The item to understand a torment point which not only causes the organization noteworthy cost, loss of business but also causes possible administrative penalties.
- The item, which is vigorous enough to rival the occupants and beat them in a no-holds-barred matchup.

The occupants use it as a misfortune head, wiping out any potential edge.

7.6.5 FINANCIALLY SAVVY MARKETING TO ATTRACT CONSUMERS

Client procurement is a noteworthy issue for new Fintech companies. Frankly, an entire book can be composed on the subject of the obtaining clients, and the strategies will differ depending upon whether the organization has B2C or B2B contributions. To sum things up, the ways Fintech organizations could showcase are:

1. Web index advertisements
2. Company website
3. Media platforms promoting
4. E-mail marketing
5. Affiliate projects
6. Press releases
7. Expert marketing
8. Videos
9. Direct mail
10. App marketing

7.6.6 GETTING EARLY ADOPTERS AND AVOIDING SLOW SALES CYCLES

Getting early income footing is basic to decide whether the underlying item advertised is fit. Thus, early adopters are significant.

An excessive number of organizations do not develop hierarchically and remain deals pioneering. Setting aside the effort to set up a point-by-point advertising division and to assemble a business procedure and pipeline will pay off in the long haul. Numerous Fintech CEOs are attempting to satisfy their financial speculators, yet executing a procedure that will prompt progressively manageable development. This is the opportunity to truly comprehend item advertised is fit and to figure out what different highlights and usefulness ought to be added to meet explicit customer necessities.

Coming up next is a rundown of inquiries a Fintech organization might get from an investor. Numerous new businesses think little of their business cycle both in the planning and due tirelessness forms. Reasonable deals, new idea should arise through responses for inquiries:

A "proof of idea" prerequisite should require.

- The confirmation of idea should require.
- Payment for the confirmation of the idea.
- The measurements which decide fruitful evidence of ideas.
- Selection of the chief for the client's organization.
- The confirmation of ideas leads to income.
- Expectation in years one, two, and three.
- Highlights should be formed to go into full commercialization.
- The contending arrangements.
- Amount do clients have to pay for going after arrangements.
- On the off chance that win a client, and is a decent reference for future potential clients.
- A sensible income slope for this client.
- It requires critical inside assets to help this client.
- It is safe to say that you are wagering your organization on the correct clients.

7.6.7 CYBERSECURITY AND DATA PRIVACY ISSUES

Information protection, cyber security, and information break issues are particularly significant in the Fintech space. Fintech organizations frequently collect exceptionally classified data on people, such as social security numbers, credit card data, total assets, salary, and considerably more.

Programmers are progressively complex at illicitly getting to a Fintech organization's information. Their most recent stealth strategies have made it increasingly hard for organizations to distinguish and shield themselves from such assaults. Propelled secret reconnaissance systems permit assailants to screen and take information—frequently delicate exclusive data or methodologies—over a significant stretch of time without being identified.

Speculators in Fintech organizations might need to survey an organization's methods to ensure the information of workers, clients, and colleagues similar to the organization's systems and frameworks. Inquiries they may pose include:

- The intrinsic cybersecurity danger of the organization's plan of action.
- Organizations set up cybersecurity programs that formulate regulatory, functioning, and specialized power for relieving safety dangers.
- Organizations have suitable strategies, in addition, the very least a data security arrangement, a representative confronting worthy use approach, and information characterization and taking care of strategy.
- Organizations evaluate standard hazards and weakness and entrance testing of its frameworks.
- Organizations have committed security workforce.
- The organization plays out a yearly hazard evaluation identified with protection and cybersecurity.
- Organizations train its workers and also for contractual workers for protection and safety best exercises.
- Organizations have thorough occurrence reaction scheme that they have attempted it earlier.
- Organizations oversee seller chance.
- Organizations have a business congruity and debacle recuperation plan similar to reinforcement conventions.
- Organizations ensure physical security of its offices and resources.
- Organizations execute "sensible" specialized security controls (or conform to required models), for instance, against infection programming, encryption, get to controls, arrange checking, confirmation, and resource the board.
- Organizations have an internal danger plan for distinguishing prospective burglaries of exclusive data and licensed innovation.
- Organizations need protection sway appraisals while actualizing new frameworks or procedures.

Organizations learn from past information ruptures and know the outcomes.

7.6.8 TECHNICAL ISSUES AND COPYRIGHTS FOR FINTECH ORGANIZATIONS

Technological financial specialists are inspired by an organization's product, innovation, and hidden protected innovation. The information a financial specialists will seek include:

- The organization's innovation is separated.
- Upper hands in existing Fintech contributions.
- To recreate the organization's contribution would be simple.
- Exorbitant would completely accomplish, keep up, plus upgrade the contribution.
- The main protected innovation organization has licenses pending, patents, exchange mysteries, logo, and space tag.
- Organization's licensed innovation should be created.
- The organization's protected innovation does not damage the privileges of an outsider.
- The licensed innovation appropriately possessed by the organization, and has all workers and advisors allocated the protected innovation over to the organization.
- Earlier managers have potential case in the organization's licensed innovation.
- On the off chance that the protected innovation was created in college, by regime awards, for public domain innovation, does the organization reserve the option to utilize the innovation.
- Organization's licensed innovation should be live. (This can have significant duty results.)

7.6.9 WORK, CASH FLOWS, AND CHARGE MODEL ISSUES

Financial specialists are especially touchy for various crucial profession, income, plus cost model issues characteristic in these types of financial organizations, including:

As such, huge numbers of Fintech contributions you might notice. These are:

- Client procurement price low, high, or affordable for them.

- Enlistment process for the first-time clients is simple.
- Organization locates an adaptable method to get clients.
- By what method will the organization distinguish misrepresentation.
- On the off chance that the item or administration is embraced, is it hard for a client to change to another option.
- Capacity can agitate and can be alleviated.
- The long-haul estimation of a client.
- The long-haul estimation of the client is expanded after some time, while diminishing the expense of securing of a client.
- The item utilized by the client every month is frequent.
- The administration easy to understand enough.
- The level of client assistance is important to guarantee that the clients are satisfied.
- Progressing item improvement costs will be faced by the organization.
- The organization deals with the huge development in clients from a specialized point of view with adequate money-related results.
- The working assets should be escalated.
- The organization increases adequate funding to cover the organization's foreseen consumption rate.

While, the consumption rate gets excessively high and income low, it is generally hard for an organization to recoup. New organizations ought to maintain a strategic distance from the following accompanying costs:

- Extravagant workplaces and an excess of office space.
- Such a large number of gatherings paid for by the organization.
- Having huge deals and advertising group before item/showcase fit has been set up.
- An excessive number of pilots with huge monetary establishments without foreordained objectives/measurements that will prompt full-scale execution.
- An extensive time of item advancement before having the option to dispatch a negligibly feasible item.
- Worker pays rates tantamount to Amazon, Google, or a speculation bank.
- Long-haul authoritative duties.

- Key early consumptions for Fintech organizations ought to include the following:
  1. Building ability
  2. Item showcasing ability
  3. A strong business improvement representative
  4. Not too bad introductory office space situated in a territory where the organization can pull in top ability
  5. Administrative investigation

7.7 LEGAL WORK REQUIRED TO SET UP A NEW FINTECH ORGANIZATION

Speculators depend on a few inquiries to guarantee that these types of organizations are legal from a lawful point of view:

- The organization been appropriately composed. (Most financial specialists favor putting resources into enterprises, not LLCs.)
- The organization is fused.
- The organization focusing on significant authoritative issues.
- The organization consented to pertinent protection laws when giving stock or choices.
- The arrangement and value part between fellow benefactors been clarified.
- The organization is inconsistent with business laws. It has suitable approaches set up, for example, those denying inappropriate behavior and it acquired all proper work reports from representatives.
- The most part workers and contractual workers are required to sign Confidentiality and Invention Assignment Agreements.
- The organization finding a way to ensure itself in its client contracts (risk restrictions, the discretion arrangement in case of a debate, and so forth.).
- Key duty contemplations should be considered.
- The organization has a worker manual.
- The name of the organization or its administration represents any trademark issues, space name issues, or different issues.
- The organization executes a business value plan to boost workers.
- The organization agrees to every pertinent law and guidelines.

7.8 BIGGEST CHALLENGES OF FINTECH

As of late, Fintech has made an enormous wave, upsetting numerous business verticals, particularly the funding business. It has improved numerous features of accounts such as installments, cash loaning, riches of the executives, and that is just the beginning. This disturbance has brought about making consistent and remarkable client encounters, helping clients to comprehend and embrace Fintech without a lot of wavering (Rao, 2019).

These clients are a piece of a little subset. Outside of this subset, numerous individuals are as yet careful about tolerating Fintech as a result of numerous reasons like absence of trust, low straightforwardness, plausible security ruptures, or in light of the fact that they are substantially more alright with the customary methods for monetary exchanges.

The Fintech segment, making a mechanical unrest in the money business, does not neglect to discover its arrangement of difficulties. Right now, see what these difficulties are and how to beat them.

7.8.1 CHALLENGE #1: CREDIBILITY

This is the number one problem for any advancement, and it holds useful for Fintech as well. Since its the fund we are managing, the vast majority, despite everything, do not have the trust part to depend on Fintech to rearrange their monetary tasks. Picking up the certainty of individuals and have them to trust your item that is new, takes a great deal of time and exertion.

7.8.2 CHALLENGE #2: DISCOVERY

The discovery is that you may have a strong item that works quite well and you may have picked up the trust of a decent number of individuals who utilize your item to begin with. But should not something be said about the master plan? Now, you need something other than a bunch of individuals utilizing your item. There are more than 600 new Fintech companies in India, and how can we not overlook Fintech monsters. Getting your item found among the opposition is certainly a test.

7.8.3 *CHALLENGE #3: CUSTOMER RELATIONSHIPS*

Each business requires clients obviously. On the off chance that you need your client base to stay with your item and return, you have to ensure that you hold your clients over the long haul by building long-haul client connections.

7.8.4 *CHALLENGE #4: CYBERCRIME IN FINANCE*

In spite of the fact that banks put forth their 100% to guard information, it is difficult to shield everything from cybercrime (Kundariya, 2019).

There are such a large number of cybercrime frauds that threaten Fintech ventures, but Blockchain innovation can control this issue.

As the new ventures are coming up every day, Blockchain business needs to provide the best arrangements.

Even DLT, a, distributed record innovation, confronts genuine impediments.

7.8.5 *CHALLENGE #5: BIG DATA USE IN FINANCE*

The Big Database offers two chances and impediments for Fintech innovation suppliers.

Through online networking, client databases, and news sources the banks can serve their clients in a superior manner. Downpour for arranging the unstructured information for valuable data is little.

In this manner, information examination innovation is required to get the advantages. In addition, information examination arrangements are developed keeping in mind sensible exchanging, dangers, and increasingly money-related administrations.

7.8.6 *CHALLENGE #6: FINTECH DISRUPTION OF FINANCIAL INDUSTRY*

The small Fintech organizations that were rising not exactly 10 years prior cannot show the potential development, which was trusted at the hour of their rise.

Conversely, numerous different organizations can develop into a major firm.

This might be a result of the sporadic dispersion of Fintech advances.

Ascertaining the development capability of any organization has gotten hard.

Right now, making a Fintech Application safe and secure is an immense test.

7.8.7 CHALLENGE #7: THE BLOCKCHAIN INTEGRATION IN FINANCE

It is said that Blockchain is a key incombating against cybercrime. When we talk about money-related division, data security is not the main use of the Blockchain.

While it has just been demonstrated that Blockchain has the incentive in the assortment of speculation applications and banking, they take a shot at potential regions like an interest in banks and more secure installment exchanges. In any case, it is said that the business-wide reception of the Blockchain is very troublesome.

7.8.8 CHALLENGE #8: CROSSING THE DIGITAL DIVIDE IN FINANCIAL SERVICES

Computerized banking is not just about having a portable application; it is much more than that. It centers on digitizing the entire brand. In any case, do you think it is simple?

In the event that an organization follows better promoting effort from regular advertisement media to advanced channels, they will have the option to do so. These are the means by which they will have the option to arrive at their intended interest group right now.

The web-based life piece is significant, and the Facebook promotions and Google advertisements make work simpler. These assist you with tapping into the huge information, AI to find potential clients, and convey tweaked choices to them in a matter of moments.

Building a brand using social media is critical, and in this way, you should deal with issues as prior as would be prudent.

7.8.9 CHALLENGE #9: CLIENT EXPERIENCE IN THE FINANCIAL SERVICE

Client experience is the most significant issue that a large portion of the organizations face in the money-related administration industry.

Today, banking clients just spotlight on getting portable banking, and they could not care less whether the bank is Fintech or not.

It will require some investment and cash to acquire the progressions of the mature-age conventions. The majority of them have an open mentality.

7.8.10 CHALLENGE #10: REGULATORY COMPLIANCE IN FINANCE

As you most likely are aware, the administrative condition is ever-changing; the budgetary foundations need to confront steady difficulties.

The RegTech, being a developing industry, can assist with defeating the weight of consistency.

With the utilization of the most recent Fintech advancements to report administrative compliances, RegTech new companies can connect up the hole between the money-related help industry and their guidelines. It very well may be helpful for the process streamlining and robotized detailing and reviews.

7.8.11 CHALLENGE #11: EMPLOYEE RETENTION IN THE FINANCIAL INDUSTRY

For the monetary help industry, finding the correct representative is as troublesome as pulling in the clients.

The great capability and ability are the extraordinary blend, and it is elusive in the IT world. Furthermore, when the organization discovers them, transient work turns into a major issue.

Notwithstanding, if an organization needs to draw in and hold its workers, should change their way of thinking.

7.9 THE WORLD'S TOP 10 FINTECH COMPANIES

The main 10 Fintech organizations (Bajpai, 2019) from around the globe are given below:

- Ant Financial: China-based Ant Financial is a side project from the Alibaba Group (BABA). Formally established in 2014, it has begun from Alipay, the world's driving outsider installment stage established in 2004.
- Adyen: Established in 2006, Adyen gives organizations a solitary stage to acknowledge payments through any business direct any place on the planet. The Netherlands-based Adyen serves in excess of 4,500 organizations to process installments through versatile, online mode, or offline modes. Adyen keeps on developing at a quick pace and has a great program of clients, including, Facebook, Uber, Netflix, Spotify, L'Oreal, Burberry, Symantec, and Microsoft.
- Qudian: Established in 2014, Qudian is a China-based Fintech firm having a place with the class of loans. Qudian extensively works as an understudy small-scale credit site, a portion installment, and a speculation of the executive's stage. While in the Western nations, numerous buys are made through credit cards that permit restitution in portions, the customers in Chinese markets do not at present utilize a lot of that instrument and this made an extension for stages, for example, Qudian. The organization has shaped associations with a few internet businesses, computerized administrations, and budgetary administrations in an offer to draw in purchasers.
- Xero: Xero, one of the quickest developing "programming as assistance" organizations, was established in 2006 in New Zealand. The organization grows simple to utilize internet bookkeeping programming for independent ventures and has more than 1 million endorsers. Its item line up incorporates a full accumulation bookkeeping framework with a cashbook, robotized everyday bank takes care of invoicing, borrowers, lenders, deals assessment, and detailing.
- SoFi: SoFi calls itself "another sort of money organization" which is adopting a non-customary strategy to loaning and now riches the board. The organization is situated in San Francisco and was established in 2011 by four understudies who met at the Stanford Graduate School of Business. The organization presently offers understudy credit renegotiating, contract advances, individual advances, riches the board, and life coverage.

- Lufax: Established in 2011 and headquartered in Shanghai, Lufax is to a great extent a distributed bank and financing organization, possessed by Ping A Group with a solid nearness in China.
- Avant: Established in 2012, Avant is a U.S.-based Internet loaning platform bringing down the expenses and obstructions of obtaining for buyers. Avant is a tech organization that is devoted to making creative and useful budgetary items for all shoppers.
- ZhongAn: ZhongAn Online P&C Insurance Co., Ltd. is a Shanghai-headquartered organization that offers online business, portable installment, and financing ensures for Internet organizations and clients. The organization was established in 2013 by Alibaba Executive Chairman Jack Ma, Tencent Chairman Pony Ma, and Ping An Insurance Group Co. of China Ltd Chairman Ma Mingzhe.
- Klarna: Klarna is a Swedish organization that started its excursion in 2005. It started with its concentration to make Internet shopping simpler and bother free and subsequently encouraging both purchasing and selling.
- Oscar: Oscar is a noticeable InsurTech start-up established in 2013 in the United States. By uniting protection and innovation, Oscar has taken a shot at approaches to improve the human services framework and client experience. It is doing as such by giving a straightforward and quicker clinical case process, all at insignificant expenses. Oscar is making the human services framework straightforward, productive, and financially savvy for clients. Unmistakable names, for example, Fidelity, Google Capital, and Khosla Ventures, among others are on its rundown of financial specialists. Khosla Ventures characterizes OSCAR as "another sort of medical coverage organization that is utilizing innovation to make protection straightforward, instinctive and human."

7.10 MOST PROMINENT FINTECH START-UPS IN INDIA

India's Fintech fragment has extended significantly, and the information around this industry focuses to a solid development potential going ahead (Sahni, 2019). The nation's appropriation rate for Fintech items remains at 59%, the second-most elevated pace around the world, and fundamentally higher than the worldwide normal of 33%, according to investigation by DataLabs by Inc42.

Fintech new businesses have changed trade and installments from multiple points of view in the Indian market.

Here are the top Fintech new businesses in the nation:

1. Paytm
2. Paytm Money
3. PhonePe
4. MobiKwik
5. PayU
6. ETMoney
7. PolicyBazaar
8. LendingKart
9. Freecharge
10. Mswipe
11. Ezetap
12. LoanTap
13. Billdesk
14. FINO PayTech
15. Capital Float
16. Pine Labs

7.11 CONCLUSION

In conclusion, Fintech is a rising industrial sector that utilizes the latest innovations for the development of exercises in an account using electronic means and devices. Fintech is upsetting the shape and delivery of monetary services on a lot bigger scale. It can be described as the technology that attempts to develop and robotize the utility and conveyance of money-related to services. It has been utilized by masses for banking, Cryptocurrency and Blockchain, machine learning and trading, payments, lending, and insurance functions. The Fintech sector is facing the problems, such as credibility, customer relationship, cybercrime, regulatory compliance and employee retention.

KEYWORDS

- **Fintech**
- **traditional financial methods**
- **commercial brands**
- **copyright**
- **cyber security**
- **regularity issues**

REFERENCES

Bajpai, P. The World's Top 10 Fintech Companies. Updated on Oct 13, 2019. On Investopedia, Stocks> Tech Stocks.

Calvey, M. Fintech. Merriam-Webster.com Dictionary, Merriam-Webster. https://www.merriam-webster.com/dictionary/Fintech (accessed Apr 1, 2020).

Copyright @ Consumers International 2020/Website Privacy Policy.

Copyright builtin 2019, Fintech. What is Fintech? Guide to Financial Technology.

Harroch, R. D.; Guzy, M. 10 Key Issues for Fintech Startup Companies. Contributor, All Business Contributor Group copyright by Richard D. Harrach, All rights reserved, Oct. 12, 2019, 02:00 pm. EDT.

Kagan, K. Financial Technlogy—Fintech. Investopedia. Updated Jun 25, 2019.

Kundariya, H. The challenges of Fintech Application in Modern Era—A Comprehensive Guide at Customer Think on Dec 9, 2019, Tweet in share.

Leong, K.; Sung, A. Fintech (Financial Technology): What is It and How to use Technologies to Create Business Value in Fintech Way. *Int. J. Innov. Manag. Technol.* **2018,** *9* (2), 74–78.

Lin, T. C. W. Infinite Financial Intermediation. *Wake Forest Law Rev.* **2015,** *50*, 643.

Martin, H. Fintech. Merriam-Webster.com Dictionary, Merriam-Webster. https://www.merriam-webster.com/dictionary/Fintech (accessed Apr 1, 2020).

Mention, A.-L. The Future of Fintech. *Res. Technol. Manag.* **2019,** *62* (4), 59–63.

Rao, H. 3 Biggest Challenges of Fintech and How to overcome them. On April 11, 2019.

Raznick, J. Fintech. Merriam-Webster.com Dictionary, Merriam-Webster. https://www.merriam-webster.com/dictionary/Fintech (accessed Apr 1, 2020).

Sahni, A. What are the most Successful Fintech Startups in India. On 07 Oct, 2019 on inc42.com

Sanicola, L. What is Fintech? Huffigton Post. Published online Feb 13, 2017. (accessed August 20, 2017).

Schueffel, P. Taming the Beast: A Scientific Definition of Fintech. *J. Innov. Manag.* **2017,** *4* (4), 32–54.

Schuffel, P. Taming The Beast: A Scientific Definition of Fintech. *J. Innov. Manag.* **2016,** *4* (4), 32–54.

Sraders, A. The Street, Updated Feb: 11, 2020, 3:02 PM EST- Original- March 8, 2019.
www.investopedia.com> terms> Fintech. June 25, 2019.
www.quora.com. What-is-a-Fintech-company-and-what-does-it-do?

CHAPTER 8

Inbound Marketing for Fintech

ANIRUDH PANDIT

Bhai Gurudas Institute, Sangrur, Punjab

ABSTRACT

Inbound marketing for Fintech is the need of the hour, as inbound marketing is helpful in differentiating the potential customers from just visitors and help in focusing and developing the marketing tools and techniques accordingly. Detailed step-by-step process of inbound marketing is discussed in this chapter. This chapter also throws light on various inbound marketing techniques that are administered by Fintech companies. These techniques also act as guide for Fintech start-ups. Apart from that various tools that help in Fintech marketing are also listed in this chapter. Every company either existing or new one, first go through the pros and cons of inbound marketing, before selecting methods and tools, and these are listed at the end part of the chapter. Company can apply more than one method and tool at a time, but before selecting any tool and method, it is advised to take expert advice or do extensive market research.

8.1 INTRODUCTION

In the last decade, world has shown a tremendous increase in interest in Fintech and this interest has trebled in most recent five years, this

Revolutionary Challenges and Opportunities of Fintech. Shweta Anand, PhD, Shalini Srivastav, PhD, Vikas Garg, PhD, & Geetika Garg (Eds.)

growth has profited many creative organizations due to expanded support by the bureaucracy. The quantity of organizations endeavoring to prevail in the segment has duplicated, proving to be impossible to stick off. How new financial technology companies showcase the answer for more extensive crowd when such a large number of contenders, frequently with a higher spending plan, are attempting to do likewise? Inbound is a strategy for drawing in, connecting with, and enchanting individuals to grow a business that offers some benefit and manufactures trust. As development shifts, inbound associates an approach to manage cooperating in a human and obliging way. Inbound is a better strategy than grandstand, a better technique than sell, and a better strategy than serve your customers. Since when helpful for-the-customer infers valuable for-the-business, your association can grow better as time goes on. By making content planned to address the issues and needs of your ideal customers, you pull in qualified prospects and gather trust and legitimacy for your business.

Inbound Fintech Marketing is a promoting approach concentrated on drawing in potential clients, clients and speculators through applicable, opportune and helpful substance that has an incentive at each phase of the client's excursion. From introductory association to buy, venture, ICO or sign-up, the attention is on ensuring you become something guests to your site cannot survive without. As opposed to conventional "outbound" promoting, you are not simply battling for consideration in an ocean of immaterial substance on the web but instead you are offering answers for individuals who as of now have an issue or challenge they are hoping to understand. In the event that your substance is helpful, it can and will draw in qualified leads who will confide in your image. By and large, it makes 47% bigger buys. Inbound Fintech advertising is significantly more viable than conventional marketing techniques and is the most ideal approach to transform outsiders into clients, clients and advertisers of your item. The best part? Inbound advertising should not be dependent on any one stage or any one kind of web-based promoting, and the just a single stage, it pushes all your latent capacity prompts is your site. Facebook could close down tomorrow, and this would not have too enormous of an effect to your methodology on the grounds that inbound marketing is additionally staggeringly nimble and ready to flex with changes in stages, individuals, and inside ventures.

8.1.1 INBOUND MARKETING FUNNEL

The inbound marketing funnel is the exemplary representation system to help convert potential clients to leads, consumers, and advertisers. It consists of four stages: attract, convert, close, and delight. These checkpoints or stages help us to figure out where our possibilities are in their excursion; regardless of whether they are at the top, the center or at the base of the channel. By relating a possibility's situation to an individual stage, advertisers can utilize the channel to figure out what substance to use to push these leads down the pipe and what phases of the pipe are working (or not—and afterward fix them). Along these lines, the advertising channel does these four things for you:

- Goes about as a strategy for transport, permitting to decide precisely a possibility's position.
- Give you what substance you are conveying at each phase of the pipe.
- Assist you with settling on what you have to do so as to get them from the highest point of the channel to the base—and exit as a client.
- Distinguish potential issues that may emerge in a purchaser's excursion and fix them likewise.

Before we start explaining the stages, first we should answer few questions which are given below:

- How are clients going to show up at your site?
- What they do when they arrive?
- How you are planning to convert?

Client excursion mainly rely upon the administration one give to them, how routinely one need purchasers to come back to one's administration, and what sort of purchaser are they. A moderately small worth Business-to-consumers buy will have an altogether unlike client excursion to an all the zenith worth, great haul Business-to-Business administration.

Now let us discuss the methodology for inbound marketing which consists of four steps and is summarized below:

Step one—Attract—It is a procedure of changing over aliens to plot guests. They may discover guests by an assortment of means, powered through site improvement endeavors, online life technique, content offers, PPC, and the sky is the limit from there.

Step two—Convert—Unknown guests begin to become recognizable leads through committed points of arrival, clear suggestions to take action, and contact structures to assist them with enlisting enthusiasm for what you bring to the table.

Step three—Close—The transformation step-by-step turns into a help client. This is frequently overseen through e-mail work processes which support a sole, then teach, finally exhibit what is your item/administration will accomplish for the system.

Step four—Delight—There is no stopping for the channel when the deal is made sure about. This is the place when one can persuade one's clients to turn into one's advertisers and customary clients, empowering rehash occupation by applying discussions and substance.

There are certain areas that need to be taken under consideration, while following the inbound marketing process. These areas are discussed below:

It is vital to a business that they do not race through the procedure for making a definitive Inbound Marketing objective. In any case, there are only a few things that ought to never be finished during the Inbound Marketing process.

Something else to mull over is to abstain from skipping steps. Everything should be set up for Inbound Marketing to work successfully. This incorporates tidying up your site, expelling futile content, data and symbolism, for instance. Concerning site, you need to ensure that it is advanced for versatile use. Cellphones have become gigantic substance-based promoting and ought to be used.

Having content is acceptable, however, quality substance is incredible. You need your crowd to leave with valuable data, not pointless. So also, you would prefer not to make conspicuous pages that interest somebody and just force their expectation without having great substance to back it up. It would be disillusioning for the potential possibility as it would miss the mark regarding their desires from a very much created site with little incentive to them.

As an associate, evade trivial Call-to-Actions. Call-to-Actions are in every case great to assist to accumulate with reaching data and make the extension between the organization and potential lead. You additionally need your Call-to-Actions to be noticeable, making it simple to discover for the peruser. On the off chance that you place the Call-to-Actions in an unbalanced spot, it just bodes well that the client experience will be corrupted in a manner of speaking.

8.1.2 INBOUND MARKETING METHODS

Inbound promoting has gotten progressively famous in the marketing and publicizing world throughout the previous quite a long while, and it is nothing unexpected why? While customary outbound advertisement crusades endeavor to convince new crowds with deals y messages, "inbound" battles center around the worth they can give to clients. What is more that prompts those clients to normally incline toward those business when the need emerges. For the most part, inbound promoting systems are more affordable, hold a more extensive scope of advantages, and over the long haul, will produce a higher pace of return. Along these lines, if these advantages impact you, think about the accompanying inbound marketing techniques, which are among the most well-known and are discussed as follows:

Search engine optimization (SEO)—61% of advertisers are making website improvement a main need. Essentially, site design improvement has constantly included catchphrase research and third-party referencing in different structures. In any case, as Google's calculations are changing constantly, website streamlining never stops. One thing remains however that clients scan for a solution on Google at the present time. On the off chance that you do not show up as per arrangement, you will not create numerous heads. Excellent substance is the way to compelling, enduring website streamlining—the normal word check result currently stands at 1890 for first-page. Google creeps pages on the basis of length of content, significance, power, and its effectiveness in connecting with different springs. Financial technology represents a powerful sector presenting a lot of chance for careful, reliably refreshed, esteem including content. Some of the search engine optimization (SEO) strategies that can be employed for improving online presence are as follows:

- Quality above quantity – Guarantee what you are sharing is the thing that the guest is searching for – Basic is to give fresh and up to date data and in particular, give what individuals need to know rather what you have to tell them. For instance, if an individual scans for "How one can create a bank account?" and grounds through the page on your site, adhere to giving only particular data. On the off chance that you mess the spot and have a go at selling different administrations and befuddle the guest, you will lose a client just as a decent positioning.

- Prompt readiness for customer queries—Either have an online visit choice to answer your customer requests or have a strong FAQ page. Maintain a strategic distance from a situation where a client inquiry goes un-responded and the client moves to rival's site looking for the appropriate response. Have your documentation collaboration on making inquiries in all the potential means that a client can consider for. This immediate depicts to client questions makes expanding site design improvement (SEO) for money-related administrations suppliers.
- Link-based trust building—The data you distribute on your site has connections with related eminent destinations (outbound connections), it causes Google to accept your site as another firm. Equivalent applies to different sites or URLs have connections to your site (inbound connections). Presently, how about we not get into the math of how and why, simply remember that these connections disclose to Google about other URLs that believe on your specific site for data, also your site alludes to famous wellsprings of data (Forbes, Government locales and comparative). Unwavering quality is the thing that we should concentrate on.
- Be available where your client is—Be present where your customer is—Brain picturing; clarify by pictures or designs—Reports state, 65% of us incline toward taking a gander at a picture to adapt instead of understanding content. Presumably, we take a gander at an info graphic first than high contrast content. It is subsequently prescribed for banks to share data as info graphics instead of protracted content. Extraordinarily information that you realize will be exhausting for non-investor to peruse and comprehend. You will consequently can draw in more guests, as individuals will comprehend compound financial procedures snappier and it will be engaging the peruser.
- Be obvious through substance creation—It is critical to connect with guests and be yourself progressively obvious in the event that

you need to be seen on the web. Compose writes, distribute, and enlighten through your site which draws your guest's consideration. Make a membership directory with the goal that every blog you distribute is directed to selected beneficiaries, in this manner expanding your website traffic.

- Develop an application—With the check of cell phone clients previously jumping 2 billion, need not to be abandoned without an application. Clients need for an exchange in a hurry. A versatile perfect site is acceptable to begin with however an application is a superior choice. Your opposition would have just done it and it is basic for you to perceive what one might have done extraordinary—a thin application might be or extra point, make it intuitive, develop an engaging UI and so forth. Offers must be provided regarding downloading application in return of prize or by providing limits on shopping.
- Devote time on On-Page search engine optimization (SEO)—Title tag must contain primary catchphrase with interactive connection that appears on Google hunt. Accessible watchwords are the initial ones to be looked by Google. On the other hand, your site inner URLs ought to have catchphrases just as should show the levels from the landing page for the Google calculations to know the chain of importance of each page.
- Regional search engine optimization (SEO)—Prior getting acclaim at the worldwide platform, it is imperative to cater the neighborhood clients. Clients from closer area have greater opportunity of visiting instead of somebody from an alternate place in excess of a range of 15 miles. To show your presence at local level one should do some basic things.

    a. Make sure your address and contact number is refurbished and is in accordance.
    b. Connect all the branches through map for easy search results.
    c. Make cardinal facts available like facilities, services along with contact particulars.
    d. Review yourself from existing customers.

Blog—nearly 47% of likely purchasers shall peruse between three to five bits of substance prior thinking about addressing a business consultant.

There are three significant advantages of blogging—First is assisting marque with positioning in terms of searching, guarantees normal content refreshment, then conveys the guests that you have an idea head in your area. In any event, a long-time old blog sections and repurposing them can grow common traffic by 111%. Key for building up a financial technology blogging methodology is arranging. Tapping in watchword search leads in discovering, explicit torment focuses as well as issues one can pinpoint. Discover what is a rival are progressing admirably and what is

Onlooker's redirect—Those clients who watch redirect advertisements comprises off 70%, bound to change over in light of the fact that they are as of now acquainted with your image, and 26% of all out retargeted guests will change over. When you are not redirecting, possibly you are overlooking an immense measure of probable clients. By utilizing treats on your webpage, you can monitor your site traffic and target promotions through web-based life as well as network-based display on Google. These clients will undoubtedly become reward clients. More filtered the redirecting; one can adjust more important publicizing for more applicable in gathering the clients, expanding odds of change.

Pay per click (PPC) ads—It is natural in inbound marketing that clients find you, instead of expressly offering to clients. In any case, PPC advertisements is yet a compelling method to target prospects over an assortment of diverts when utilized in mix with inbound. Exceptionally focused on PPC advertisements can expand lead changes by half contrasted with absolutely natural traffic, and 52% of web-based business customers will tap on PPC promotions. Whenever focused on well, they can show up directly before potential clients after preparing the replies for the inquiries. Dealing with an account of PPC adequately implies adjusting catchphrase intensity, disseminating spending plan viably, composing the most convincing promotion duplicate, and connecting to the most focused on greeting pages.

E-mail marketing—Had not one realized that the clients purchasing via e-mail burn through 138% higher than the individuals who had not? That is on the grounds that instead of outbound advertising, where one is attempting to go however fresh individuals could be allowed—together with a huge rate of individuals who are not keen on what you bring to the table—inbound marketing through e-mail centers around constructing associations and distinguishing as possible as first position, for instance, by focusing on explicit purchaser personas, utilizing personalization and making shareable substance to impart your skill.

Video marketing—Organizations utilizing broadcasting for speaking to their clients become 49% quicker than other organizations that are not using this. Nothing unexpected: video is an incredible method to transverse important data in an animating manner, and more importantly, one can utilize this nearly for anything! Regardless of you need to give your customers a demo of your new budgetary thing, or you're searching for an approach to advance your organization by providing the clients a look off camera of what goes on at your workplaces, video can undoubtedly make an enthusiastic association and urge individuals to consider you to be the correct item or administration.

Social media marketing—Nearly, half of business-to-business purchasers search an organization data via web-based networking media before making a buy. Media is an incredible method to draw in both new and bringing customers back. To put forth your web-based life inbound marketing attempts a triumph you have to depict yourself as a specialist or suspected pioneer in your field, and an extraordinary method to do this is through the creation and advancement of incredible substance, regardless of via claimed (devoted social channels), paid (promoting) or earned online life (increased by sharing by others and discussing one's substance).

Brand enactments—Brand enactment is tied in with making one's image name "out there." At the point when you initially began your organization, nobody realized you were: you needed to "actuate" yourselves by advancing your image and giving your potential clients an essential encounter. Brand enactment does not stop once you are fully operational; however regardless of whether it is marketing through experiments, testing efforts or in-store brand actuation, you ought to consistently be searching for approaches that make your image stuck in somebody's mind. It will become clear in one mind long before what is best; however, it is prescribed to utilize a blend of the above-mentioned.

A whitepaper—The definition and motivation behind a whitepaper relies upon who you inquire. The business you are in and the objectives you seek after positively impact the last item. A whitepaper as a top to bottom, all around looked into a bit of instructive substance that receives to some degree more proper tone than your normal blog entry. While a blog entry is your week after week schoolwork task, a whitepaper is your research paper. When in doubt, accept that the possibilities who download your whitepaper are anticipating higher degrees of meticulousness, profundity, inventiveness, and worth. The key preferred position of a whitepaper over a blog entry or an info graphic is that—notwithstanding offering some benefit to the individuals who fit the bill for your item or administration—you can require contact data in return.

An ebook—The advantages of a digital book are entirely like those of a whitepaper. It is another chance to build up your image as a definitive asset of noteworthy, clever data. Commonly, it is for nothing out of pocket and traded for contact data. In the event that you choose to join digital books into your inbound system—and I do prescribe it—do not trifle with the errand. Keep in mind: You are composing a book. That suggests a really genuine degree of modernity. You should save this substance group for your really hard-hitting material.

A case study (or customer spotlight)—Think that you are an entrepreneur in the market for an internet-based social media software company. While you are perusing the blog of one of the organizations you are thinking about, you go over a contextual investigation. It recounts to the narrative of an organization—frightfully like yours—that purchased the product a year back and has seen positive returns from that point forward. This product has had a colossal effect for the highlighted client. Normally, you contemplate internally: "Well that implies it can work for me, as well, right?" That's the intensity of a contextual analysis. It exhibits to the individuals going back and forth that your item or administration has done miracles for individuals simply like them.

A webinar—A webinar (online course) is a web workshop—addresses style content introduced to a selective web crowd. With this organization, a part (or a couple of individuals from) your substance group has the chance to give that important data and do it in a profoundly captivating and amicable manner. The nearness of a genuine, conscious individual—regardless of whether it is simply their voice—makes the inclination that your image is in direct discussion with your possibilities. While it is simple for your possibilities to extract away the gifted individuals who make your blog entries, whitepapers, and digital books, that is not the situation with an online course. Also, by and by, the capacity to demand data from your possibilities as an extra charge makes the webinar (online course) an especially decent lead age strategy.

A podcast—Much like the online course, the digital recording group permits you to join some character to your image. That way, when your possibilities are settling on their official conclusions, they will recollect you as both an important and relatable asset. Podcasting should not be work serious, either. In the event that you have a PC, a couple mikes, and at any rate, one collaborator who sounds like Steve Buscemi, you are ready to go. One 30-minute scene 7 days is everything necessary to turn into the drawing in brand potential clients go to, during their Monday regularly scheduled drives.

A video series—Video content being a gigantic industry, developing and connecting with, and in particular, it is compelling. It is what individuals need to see when they are looking through Facebook and Instagram. It breathes life into your image. Video is best, when it is reduced down, is littler as online life clients are commonly uninterested in recordings that go longer than a moment or two. Video is an incredible chance to repurpose content in an increasingly absorbable arrangement. A possibility might not have had the opportunity to go to your online class, yet he can most likely extra two minutes while looking through LinkedIn to get the fundamental thoughts.

8.1.3 INBOUND MARKETING TOOLS

There are a huge amount of instruments that are constructed explicitly to help with specific parts of inbound promoting. We have assembled a rundown of a portion of the top inbound promoting apparatuses:

HubSpot—Development programming offering lead age, advertising computerization, and the sky is the limit from there. HubSpot has more than 40,000 clients across 90 nations, and perhaps the best instrument accessible. HubSpot is one of the pioneers of inbound advertising apparatuses. There is everything in-one suite of inbound advertising programming that will empower a solitary individual to play out crafted by a whole marketing group.

Google Adwords—Internet publicizing over Google system, if a website guest clicks on to your advertisement or enquires through your promotion, you would possibly pay for that. Publicize all around or locally and show up in focused, significant quests.

Analytics—Analytics works by measuring guest on particular site, find where and when they are vacating you, and how they discover regardless. These experiences are critical for estimating the achievement of inbound technique.

Leadfeeder—It lets you know precisely who is visiting your site by introducing the Leadfeeder Tracker content and interfacing with Google Analytics to help distinguish the organizations from your mysterious site guests. At that point it improves this information to give contact data to key possibilities at those organizations and permits you to adjust your prompts with various CRM and mechanization devices. Following your site guests on a record level is a significant strategy that suits well with any inbound advertising methodology. Via naturally recognizing your mysterious site guests, you can fill your business pipeline with drives you never realized you had _and_ better screen and investigate your current inbound marketing endeavors.

Drift – Drift takes nearby client cooperation to the following level by utilizing live visit boxes and savvy bots to prequalify leads and prospects before they are sent to your business group. Evaluating is free for singular clients, $50/month for a standard arrangement, and $500/month for an endeavor account.

ProProfs Survey Maker—It is an incredible device to praise your inbound advertising methodology. This apparatus permits you to make adjustable popup structures to transform site guests into leads and reviews to assemble explicit data about your potential clients. The top to bottom reports assist you with understanding which pop-ups will assist you with catching more guests, eye-based, on which you can additionally upgrade your inbound advertising methodologies.

Survey Monkey—Looking over your clients is an extraordinary method to get information that can be utilized to settle on business choices. Survey Monkey empowers you to accumulate knowledge and afterwards, investigates it utilizing worked-in incredible information examination apparatuses. The information you assemble would then be able to be utilized to make a substance promoting technique.

Canva—This spellbinding instrument lets you make proficient structures for your battle regardless of whether you have little plan capacity. Your group can utilize it to produce specially crafts, info graphics, web-based life pictures, eBooks, introductions, and online life profile headers—without pestering a visual originator. Canva accompanies a wide scope of free and paid pictures and layouts.

Hotjar—Monitoring client experience on your site is basic to compelling inbound promoting. The Hotjar device lets you increase important input from your site guests. This apparatus creates heat maps, criticism surveys, transformation channel investigation and information demonstrating how guests draw in with your site. Hotjar accompanies a free bundle, just as a paid alternative with more highlights.

Click To Tweet—Making quality substance, some of the time it is not sufficient in advertising—you need that substance to reach, however, many individuals could be expected under the circumstances. The free Click To Tweet causes you make Tweet-able connections that your Web guests can then effectively use to share your substance. You should simply make appealing "Click To Tweet" boxes anyplace inside your posts featuring explicit messages or statements. Perusers would then be able to tap on the source of inspiration catch to in a flash offer your message. Other than Web content, you can likewise utilize "Click To Tweet" to advance your blog entries, white papers, eBooks, and messages.

Flow—This is another extraordinary device for errand and tasks of the executives. Stream permits you to list significant errands, organize them in a like manner and agent them to your colleagues. To plan your assignments, you should simply relocate them into your schedule. You can likewise design ventures, talk about undertakings and get criticism from your group—across-the-board place.

8.1.4 PROS OF INBOUND MARKETING

Cold pitching—a type of outbound advertising—is finished. Rather, the development of web crawlers, more prominent customer decision, and the instantaneousness of advanced arrangements have brought about inbound advertising turning into the best computerized marketing technique to draw in new career.

1. Less cost—61% of the cost leads inbound not exactly outbound leads all things considered, normal expense per lead dips by 80% following 5 months of revealing an inbound system. Web journals, internet-based life and natural pursuit content is the absolute best systems in the arena of Fintech, further least expensive to deliver.
2. Customer trust building—As per research of Business-to-business chiefs preferring doing self-exploration. Important, instructive substance gives customers the data they truly need, helping them settle on an educated choice about your image and stay faithful.

3. Making Fintech start-up a progressively reasonable choice for financial specialists—Significant financial specialists need to "comprehend the item being built...and how adaptable it is." A successful inbound promoting system creates, develops, supports leads, and transform them into long-haul clients.
4. Develops fruitful data—Inbound crusades give fragmented, astute information, further utilized for comprehending needs and practices of current and prospect clients. Supported leads purchase 47% higher than regular purchase.

8.1.5 CONS OF INBOUND MARKETING

In spite of the fact that there are numerous geniuses to Inbound Marketing, a couple of cons can join the region too. Although Inbound Marketing can be financially savvy, it does not mean that the expense is inside an organization's spending limit. Inbound requires a great deal of exertion and expertise to make a compelling effort that possibilities can connect appropriately and be fulfilled. It is a dedication that the organization should completely participate in to end up as the winner with this strategy. Commonly, it takes an enormous group to finish a full Inbound Marketing strategy. Scholars, strategists, creation groups, and originators, for instance, on the off chance that you can discover a stage that can locate an across-the-board stage, you can decrease the cons to making significant Inbound substance.

8.2 CONCLUSION

Generally, business people and financial specialists went cap close by to the bank to apply for a home loan, private company credit line or money market fund, yet, now Internet and long-range interpersonal communication shape our everyday choices, clients are presented to more data than any time in recent memory. Budgetary innovation, or Fintech, is quickly changing all that by making it simpler to spare, acquire, and contribute on the web or with a cell phone, while never managing a customary bank. This wonder is not just making them increasingly instructed, yet, additionally is causing an adjustment in purchasing practices. This change has grabbed the eye of controllers, shopper promoters and industry veterans—some cheering, others booing, yet all pondering:

- Will a digitized monetary administrations industry mean lower costs, more advancement and more noteworthy access for all?
- Or on the other hand, will the prevailing players at last remain on top, with their powerful expenses, bonuses and pay, just as their watchman jobs, to a great extent flawless?

Subsequently, B2B and B2C advertising endeavors must be changed in accordance with the reaction to this changed behavior. The current associations comprehend that the outbound undertakings alone are inadequate to make benefits. Or maybe, inbound advertising methodologies ought to be utilized in order to attract more leads and develop better brand tendency. To be productive in inbound advertising, associations need to familiarize a showed approach with content creation, present advancing motorization gadgets that can help them with supporting and score leads, and advance how these leads course through the business pipeline, But make sure to consistently deliver quality and valuable substance for your focused on customers.

KEYWORDS

- **inbound marketing methods**
- **marketing tools**
- **business-to-business**
- **inbound advertising**
- **content creation**

REFERENCES

https://www.digitalauthority.me/resources/Fintech-marketing-strategies/
https://webbuzz.com.au/digital-marketing-services/Fintech-marketing/
https://2muchcoffee.com/blog/marketing-strategies-for-Fintech-startup/
https://www.clickz.com/7-rules-a-Fintech-must-follow-to-succeed-with-its-marketing-strategy/260419/

https://www.inboundFintech.com/complete-guide-to-inbound-marketing-for-Fintech-startups-inbound-Fintech#the_benefits_of_inbound_marketing
https://startupflux.com/10-digital-marketing-seo-strategies-for-Fintech-startups-to-improve-their-presence-online/
https://www.meticulosity.com/blog/Fintech-needs-inbound-marketing
https://www.responsify.com/what-does-inbound-mean-inbound-marketing-funnel/#Pros%20and%20Cons%20of%20Inbound%20Marketing
https://www.wordstream.com/blog/ws/2018/11/05/inbound-marketing-examples
https://www.kunocreative.com/blog/tools-for-inbound-

CHAPTER 9

Internal Marketing and Employee Motivation Builds Psychological Ownership in Fintech Emotional Intelligence in Industry 4.0

JYOTI KUKREJA

Jagannath International Management School, Kalkaji, New Delhi

ABSTRACT

"Appreciate or abuse, love or lose" is now an obvious choice to organizations, employees, and customers alike. Business of any shape and size expects super normal profits to itself not year on year, or quarter by quarter but perennial.

This chapter discusses about the various behavioral patterns and changes of employees in service sector. It also discusses of how both public and private banks help their staff to work for the benefit of their organization. The survey included employees at frontline and managerial level from banking industry in Delhi, capital of the country, India. Findings of the study are interesting and are relevant with employees taking ownership with challenging job assignments and growth opportunities. Empowerment and constructive feedback ensure self-efficacy which builds opportunities for development purposes. These contribute to the escalation of higher motivational levels as antecedents to the concepts of psychological changes and inhouse marketing. Appreciative inquiry is a

Revolutionary Challenges and Opportunities of Fintech. Shweta Anand, PhD, Shalini Srivastav, PhD, Vikas Garg, PhD, & Geetika Garg (Eds.)

concept that is based on making good and positive strings stronger for higher productivity in the organization.

9.1 INTRODUCTION

This study is based on the exploration of the concept of employee motivation and internal marketing practices in the banking industry. The aspect of psychological ownership implies taking control over things and people. The feeling of being a proprietor requires sub-dimensions of self-confidence, self-esteem, and autonomy. The results deliver contribution to the academic theory and managerial decision-making capabilities.

Considering employees equivalent to customers can increase the trust and feeling of commitment and loyalty to a large extent. This concept of internal marketing helps in making business sustainable. An organization needs a talent pool to operate and excel. Succession through various market challenges requires strengths and capabilities of its employees. All stakeholders require growth which is possible not only with the enhancement of competencies and skills set of those who function inside the organization but also of those who patronize the products and services. Thus, customers need to be educated with the multiple dimensions of the existing offerings so that the market share expands. What will happen if an organization innovates new services such as ATM or digital payment but its customers do not use it? To make new practices and innovation successful, it is essential that the management in its purview keeps not only the employees but also about customers for success. This is required to ensure that the market accepts the product manufactured and does not ignore the innovation. This thereby implies that success of the industry and organization depends on customers who are dependent on employees for rendering high-quality services and vice versa where employees manufacture considering the viewpoints of employees. Psychological ownership means taking control and autonomy over the organizational resources and customer experiences. The feeling of assuming responsibilities beyond a particular job designation requires self-assumed roles to empower over the results as made explicit by the organizations in comparison to the competitors. Customers' expectations need to be taken into account because that determines the success of the enterprise.

In the globalized world of today, creativity that is not only solution to the problem at hand but easy and design featured which is interesting to use and apply. Organizations can achieve their mission only when market expectations are super exceeded. The creative potential of individuals collectively forms the strength of organizations. The creative potential can only be constituted with the competencies and enhanced skills strength of its employees and also suggestions from customers. Training and development of the staff ensures building their psychological well-being. Subjective well-being of an individual is dependent on the mindset of an individual. The increase in technical expertise of an employee is based on the skills session attended and practiced at the workplaces.

For an employee to be motivated, it is essential to ascertain high pedestal of a psychology so much so that an employee is not there for the execution of allocated work but for creating something new in the given organizational ecosystem and climate. The extra-role behavior, such as active listening to the customer queries patiently and making them smile once they leave the counter to ensure customer delight are not mentioned in their job profiles, but once they take upon their roles and designation and hold them dearly to themselves, the productivity of the organization can be enhanced manifold. Kotler remarked that for a committed customer, it is essential to entail employees' organizational commitment.

As an HR Manager, I give training and development workshops on time management, prioritizing, and scheduling assignments to increase productivity. But these outcomes are just momentary, and the struggle to accomplish both job and organizational productivity is an enigma that hovers on top management.

Organizations cannot guarantee success if it lacks appreciative inquiry. It is not essential to focus on the gray zones but to focus on the areas of brightness. Many a times, recommendations and strategies are based out of deficiency zones which engender negativity. This negativity in turn breeds inferiority. This inferiority makes the existence rather more complex and abstruse thereby causes employees to suffer from stress. Subsequently, anxiety spruces up not only nurture pessimism but also will snowball the similar effect on other departments and branches.

To overcome this shadow effect of tension in the organizational climate, an extension of the concept of appreciative inquiry in the context of internal marketing is advised here. The latter is getting strong impetus from digital zone. In the internet era of today where every employee is connected to a few hundred contacts, whistle blowing could be a more intense problem to solve for managers than any of the times ever before. Thus, every digital footprint can be monitored.

It had been observed as a human tendency that negativity captures more intensely over people . Therefore, appreciation is needed in huge quantum. Appreciation, as a precursor, requires a feeling of oneness or empathy. This psychological ownership is based on the premise of taking responsibility and accountability of the tasks, decisions, people, and processes. Empowerment is the new power to the generation ahead of 4G network. Although a variety of courses and circumstances instill the need and confidence for the people to be equipped with certification and skills, yet deficiency in self-efficacy exists. But once employees are treated fairly and they believe themselves to be the owners of the organization, they would appreciate the product and its processes on their own.

In services sector, taking ownership is as difficult as catching hold of one's own shadow and passing the buck is a commonplace scenario. A commitment must be engaged with the organizational value system and its vision is then a must. The belief that the psychological contract of continuing the work processes with efficiency and effectiveness is not just a matter of choice but that of priority.

9.2 BUILDING PSYCHOLOGICAL OWNERSHIP

Psychological ownership is about assuming the role of being a judge, an arbitrator, fully responsible and accountable for considering oneself as the owner of the role that one performs. This begets better productivity to the respective department. Training and development sessions in the organizations are all aimed at enhancing the motivational and morale of employees by making them responsible and holder of their designations to the role of employees in owning organizations. It is a mode of imparting work ethics and integrity to organization. The feeling of unity in staff is possible when all employees work as a team. Organizational commitment, effective internal communication, strategic rewards, strategic leadership, vision awareness, and employee training and development are all crucial when it comes to building and engendering unity in organizational fabric.

Organizations just like people are aspiring to get lean. Though the headcount is being reduced, but emotions in people are waging a war against each other. There exists a cut throat competition as everyone is vying against each other. Since it gets narrow at the top, thus, for one to be dexterous in all aspects is highly crucial. It is not only multiple skills but multiskilling with multitasking is the route to get at the peak.

Thus, employees to be competent to sail through the turbulent changes must feel as owners. For the ownership to build up, it is essential that employees and their emotions are handled with utmost care. Nevertheless, employees do get hurt and feel victimized, thus care and cure must go hand in hand. More often than not struggles are of emotional tangent and cause impediments in execution of tasks and limit growth objectives of the departments and enterprises.

While number of MBAs is increasing, it is implied that more people want to do jobs. Why the practice then ought to continue to provide extra incentives and perquisites. At the time of recruitment, it is the candidates who themselves volunteer to appear for the interview and attempt to ace. Internal marketing is getting complex especially in the services sector where all promises made by the brand are delivered by service personnel. If jobs are sold as products to employees in the similar ways that products are sold to customers, meaning thereby that employees are wanting to and are motivated to perform and abide by organizational duties and roles, then the task of appreciative inquiry would not only become more facile but the need to incentivize to work more and with greater positivism will also need less effort to be exercised. Since, optimum utilization of resources is one of the key areas of management thus fostering an organizational climate in such a way would yield profitable results.

Servant leadership is the new oxymoron in the service sector which was introduced as a concept by in the year 1970. High levels of motivation and morale of employees are crucial for the firm to serve the existing standards of excellence and to enhance the quality further.

Motivation can be sourced from two parallel sources: internal and external. Altruism, orientation for achievement, control and power along with confidence toward self-efficacy and empowerment are internal sources of motivation, while salary, bonus, and avenues for promotion have been found to be effective external sources of motivation.

It had been found that there exists a difference between the personality types, areas of interest, and levels of motivation. Self-confidence is recognition of the fact that one is mentally and physically capable to do a task or a job.

Appreciative inquiry could best yield results if the strategy of knowledge sharing is implemented. The humanistic perspective is critical to build the psychological capital in the department and thereby in the organization.

Knowledge management is essential for knowledge sharing and enhancement of the processes toward achieving excellence in processes, employees, and branding. To build a brand, an organization needs to woo customers from the competitors, likewise they need to source employees from the rivals.

There is none who will for their first choice want the second best to themselves whether it is a personal buying decision or for organizations. It had been evident from the past literature that appreciation just like complaining nature is a habit, and until and unless a planned effort is exerted from the top management, positivity to the organization would not flow. Thus, it is essential to deploy internal marketing strategies in organization.

The benefits of appreciative inquiry are more than one. Building an employer as a brand and reducing the acquisition and retention cost of personnel are a few of the perennial advantages of the implementation of the concept.

This study shall seek to discuss in detail the relationship of employee motivation juxtaposed in the bank domain due to performance of the practices, such as customer orientation and consideration of employees as customers. This chapter shall be an exploration and description of the level of emotional competencies of the service personnel in the money depository institutions. This study survey is a result of the respondents gauged from Delhi, capital of the nation, India.

Workplaces today have a set of employees with diversity in skill sets, background, experience, and behavior. Responding and reciprocating to this heterogeneity is a challenge. The underlying principle to the concept is considering "employees equivalent to customers" and designing and selling "jobs similar to products" to them as organizations would do it to their customers.

The world has become too dynamic for any of us to calculate and envision change, yet, it is still essential to be ready to overcome it because a full lifetime is spent maintaining in an industry. Among all the industries in service sector, banking is considered to be most vibrantly circulating cash flow to all industries. Banks face competition from its own branches and employees are transferred. This creates a need to have a large talent pool.

For business of any size invariably across industries, it is crucial to have not only dedicated employees but subsequently a loyal customer database. Internal marketing is a strategy crafted and implemented to ensure consistent business.

IM is reflected through phrases, such as "This is my organization," "We empathize with your inconveniences," "I have to work toward enhancement of brand image of my organization and productivity of my department."

9.3 LITERATURE BACKGROUND

"How much do I feel this organization is mine?" Obligations, duties, and responsibilities for jobs and tasks represent ideal-self. Psychological ownership is a concept which is based on self-assumed responsibilities. It emanates from within and cannot be enforced upon. Fuchs et al. (2010) explained that psychological ownership leads to better understanding and word of mouth for all stakeholders. The demand for a product is generated when the customer has already considered themselves to be a proud and happy user. Ahmed and Rafiq (2003) mentioned this as one of the strongest competencies of the organization which helps them to command market share. Mowday et al. (1982) mentioned commitment as a psychological dimension that acts as a unison of both head and heart. An employee in service sector must experience this cohesion of logic and feeling before generating results of the task for their individual and workplace efficiency. Better and progressive decisions along with decreased absenteeism from work and reduced turnover intentions are the key results of psychologically committed service personnel. It is those who are committed are the ones who are motivated to work and perform according to rules and policies of the organizations. Malhotra and Mukherjee (2003) reported that it is essential in service industry to have committed service personnel. Disbelief cannot generate business. Therefore, the record of commitment from employees is a prerequisite to obtain commitment from customers. Deriving a competitive advantage is not easy for any firm especially in an industry which is more or less similarly characterized (Kukreja, 2019b). All banks operate under the control of RBI and have almost the same rate of interest on savings and deposits need to find out heterogeneity in the homogeneity of services. Lead in the lean organizational hierarchy structure is difficult. Greene et al. (1994) mentioned through their research that psychological ownership precedes both internal marketing and employee motivation. External success can be promised through an inside out approach.

Ahmed and Rafiq (2003) summarized that for organizations to be competent, it is essential to make employees empowered and self-capable of enhancing their capacities via continual training and development. They mentioned that only an empowered employee feels committed and motivated to become an owner. Ownership is a creation of mindset that the resources are personal to me assuring their zero-wastage should be my top most priority. Fullerton (2003) revealed that commitment and loyalty are different and the former must precede the latter. Employees may be committed but the moment they find a better job they may quit; while commitment is with no decision to leave, loyalty is finding host of options and still deciding to sustain.

IM suggests a panacea in the form of having customer-conscious employees at all levels in the organization (Gronroos, 1985), service-minded to achieve organizational excellence. For business of any size invariably across industries, it is crucial to have not only dedicated employees but also subsequently a loyal customer database. Internal marketing is a strategy crafted and implemented to ensure consistent business with service quality. Berry (1981) proposed having high-quality buyer–seller relationship. "Willing behavior and contributions of staff to achieve a given task" is defined as motivation. The enumeration of interest, personal pleasure, and delight are highlighted as the drivers of intrinsic motivation. Lings and Greenley in 2005 unfolded the aspects of internal market orientation where each employee irrespective of their department or hierarchy in the organization needs to be customer-minded. Having an approach to serve customers is essential because they are the nucleus around whom the entire processes of the organization revolve. It is essential to keep employees engaged to ensure that the productivity and thereby profits are obtained. Their study highlighted the relevant aspects of vision and mission of the organization which frame the mentality of the employees in the organization. While organizational profits are one of the few benchmarks of excellent organizational services, yet the focus on enhancing tools for their motivation and ownership of the firm will ensure that there are no employees but organizational beneficiaries working for the process of delivering customer satisfaction and better experience. Herrington and Lomax (2005) in their research answered the question in affirmation raised by them as whether satisfied employee can engender a committed customer. The research reiterated the fact that it is challenging to engage employees and more difficult to make a customer committed. This is because while employees are trained and developed and compensated for rendering their services, yet customers who are trading their payment for availing services could have made a conscious choice and decision to indulge with any of the providers need reasons beyond money to sustain. Reasons such as psychological commitment can leverage the organizations with moderate to high endurance zone for any inconveniences or troubles from customers. Emotional connect is another reason where the customer starts thinking with heart for the organizations. The techniques of relationship management can enrich the business from customers. Voluntary retention of customers is quintessential for organizations and employees to continue to sustain. Joe (2008) reported through their research that culture of learning exponentially enhances skills of employees and make them confident and self-reliant. Leader–Member Exchange Quality enhances which helps in the development of an individual. Turnover Intention is diminished to the extent of zilch if psychological commitment and ownership is raised to a level where it is felt that it is not the organizational staff, but the extended family of the individual and the organization, a second home. The leaders need to exchange qualitative thoughts with their teams to develop them with agility and proficiency. The leadership style to a very large extent decides on the significance of education and development of both team and organization. Organizational deficiencies are suspended with the leaders' capacity and competencies. For any leader, it is essential to frame their organization best among their competitors for the successful return of their customers.

9.4 RESEARCH MODEL

The previous studies contribute toward market share building and retention.

A conceptual model was designed to vividly portray both the antecedents and outcomes of levels of penetration of internal marketing. It had been scooped from the literature review that organization culture, management philosophy, orientation to customers, policies and procedures, and internal market orientation are predecessors to the breeding of motivational aspects of behaviors that form psychological commitment of employees. It is more than important in today's competitive scenario to score an edge and build market share where services are perceived to be homogeneous due to standardization. The application of internal marketing yields outcomes at two levels, that is, immediate benefits, such as role clarity, higher levels of employee motivation, service quality, employee commitment, and integration and coordination. To further advance, the second level outcomes of internal marketing, such as organizational performance, customer satisfaction, employee engagement, accelerated change management as a process, and low employee work stress are the series of advantages culminated.

Internal marketing factors, such as training and development, organizational support, incentives and motivation, and retention policy are examples of the independent variables. Employee motivation is a representation of the dependent variable. A thorough review of the literature in the banking sector, in particular, has resulted in the development of the following framework model for research: At the first-level outcome, implementation of the concept of IM would generate achievement of role clarity, enhancement of motivation and morale of employees, escalation in the quality of services being delivered, voluntary retention of employees as a conscious, and willful decision expedite to eradicate any delay in business processes. IM acts as a lubricant that works to integrate and coordinate with all departments.

With the concept of internal marketing in practice, employees are considered to be customers to the organization. IM is being used by the most successful enterprises in various industries as a means to enhance productivity. Internal communication, training and development, and education toward organization, team, and individual goals as a tripod tool accelerate and facilitate the implementation of internal marketing process.

9.5 RESEARCH QUESTIONS

The study is a unique attempt to explore the relation between appreciative inquiry, psychological ownership, and internal marketing. Independent variables of the concept of employees' motivation which includes self-efficacy, psychological contract, organizational commitment and an orientation for appreciative inquiry proved useful for understanding the best behavior and interests of service personnel.

- If employees feel unison with the organization due to factors, such as good rewards?
- Can recognition help improve the appreciative inquiry index of the organization?
- What dimensions of psychological ownership can impact on employees?
  - H1: Internal marketing propels employee motivation
  - H2: High levels of employee motivation ensure implementation of internal marketing
  - H3: Internal marketing influences psychological ownership
  - H4: Psychological ownership builds appreciative inquiry in the organization

The suggested study aims to examine the internal marketing programs and tactics employed by participants in the country's main banks. It will also attempt to investigate the causes and effects of such internal marketing initiatives. The study would pay particular attention to the effect, if any, that internal marketing initiatives may have on employee motivation. It is also possible to investigate the connection between internal marketing strategies and staff churn. It would also investigate any connections, if any, between internal marketing techniques, employee motivational interventions in banks, and organizational development and profitability. One such sector where changes in the macroenvironment and brain drain have occurred frequently is banking. About two-thirds of the workers rejected reform in the 1990s and opted for the golden handshake. The human resources were thus put at risk.

9.6 RESEARCH MODEL

The research model shows that psychological ownership through constructive feedback is a powerful communication tool can build employee motivation. All these endeavors are targeted at enhancing productivity of both the individual department and organizations. These three concepts are designed toward customer relationship management. A customer would also feel ownership and belongingness to the firm if there is oneness with the firm. It is necessary for employees to feel one with the company and the same feeling to be created among customers. When the customers report their association with the company as "mine," it can escalate the image perception of the brand to the next level and make the new employees more motivated and dedicated for the organizational processes. Empowerment and autonomy over the people (in the form of both employees and customers) can give the feeling of self-confidence to the employees which are a requirement for the execution of tasks as prerequisite.

9.7 RESEARCH METHODOLOGY

Snowball sampling method was followed to gauge insights from 250 respondents, out of which 220 respondents agreed to cooperate. While 15 respondents lost the survey form 15 returned unfilled. 15 questionnaires were discarded due to incomplete information. It was found that to comprehend and identify application of the internal marketing in the background of motivation of employees empowerment, rewards, recognition, and training and development played a crucial role. Both exploratory and descriptive research had formed the basis of the analysis.

Stratified sampling method was adopted. Out of the final sample size of 175, total 85 respondents constituted of six banks of public sector and 95 respondents of six banks in private sector. The study was undertaken during a span of 4 months, September 19–December '19. The research was carried out in the areas of Delhi and NCR.

9.8 RESULTS

Young employees were reported to be more agile in terms of building customer relations and delivering according to organizational performance. Employees with less than 5 years of experience were found to be more enthusiastic toward challenging job assignments. Since they are young, there is a higher need for them to be trained and counseled on the aspects, such as soft skills namely customer handling, grievance redressal, communication, building trust, etc. Purchase of services from banks requires long-term decisions of investment. A customer might have multiple accounts but just like telecom industry, they frequently do not change their phone number and bank account number.

It was conveniently found that employee motivation is a cause of internal marketing as a concept to flourish and to be implemented. Subsequently, prevalence of internal marketing practices, such as employee training and development along with job satisfaction are long-term visionary ideas that believe that people often need to drive work. Loyalty is another key area of concern. This is because of the fact that people are least wanting to commit themselves to a particular work, and even if they do, they are divided in terms of multiple profits that they think could be sourced from different contracts. The contracts that are built up and sustained are based on the cases and causes of durability of profit. It had been well established that high levels of customer-mindedness and sales-consciousness result in smooth inter-functional integration and feeling of belongingness, and the spirit of unity causes a collective approach to overcome organizational resistance for accepting and channelizing change. The stronger and thicker the bond of espirit-de-corps in the staff, higher the autonomy and feeling of self-efficacy, fulfillment, and empowerment and autonomy which all equates to higher levels of psychological ownership that further enhances organization as a united whole than several segregated and bifurcated units.

9.9 CONCLUSION

Fear is one of the strong elements of motivation. During the survey among bank personnel, it was found that employees who were apprehensive of losing their jobs performed more. Not only this, significant level of morale and motivation that made them was more positive than others found in the survey.

Challenge is another strong element that is known to keep employees electrified and motivated. An attitude to dare to face the unknown, the courage to take up tasks that others avoid have been known to provide better package and aura to the person. The ambition avenues that are escalating in the career ladder had been found to be more attainable to employees who were either more competent or skillful. An alternative category to the above is a set of employees who are more confident beyond their limitations and weaknesses.

During the times of demonetization, Indian economy went through a distressed phase. A time of lot of stress and anxiety with a lot of financial worries caused a huge economic turmoil in all households of the country. Every individual learnt to respect each penny that they beheld and money became both an instrument of exchange for convenience to the extent of being wishful of spending and saving at the same behest. There were a few banks in the locality which found it comfortable to turn the customers away with no money in their hands or at the ATM.

All the above stated hypotheses stand relevant. Internal marketing takes employee motivation ahead and in turn high levels of motivation aid in the implementation of the concept of internal marketing. Further psychological ownership begets positive results for organizations in the form of employees' enhanced willingness for taking up training and delivering for their job roles and performing for extra job roles and performance. Appreciative inquiry makes employees analyze positive aspects of organizations and builds ownership with the organization.

9.10 RECOMMENDATIONS

Employees' psychological ownership emanates from empowerment and autonomy which are regulated through self-governance practices. The three concepts when put together can lead to building positive word of mouth and voluntary customer retention. The grounds for compassion for building and enhancing brand image for the organization can do wonders for a firm.

KEYWORDS

- **internal marketing**
- **employee motivation**
- **banking**
- **jobs**

REFERENCES

Ahmed, P. K.; Rafiq, M. Internal Marketing and the Mediating Role of Organizational Competencies. *Eur. J. Mark.* **2003,** *37* (9), 1221–1241.

Berry, L. The Employee as a Customer. *J. Retail Bank.* **1981,** *3* (1), 25–28.

Fuchs, C.; Emanuela, P.; Martin, S. The Psychological Effects of Empowerment Strategies on Consumers' Product Demand. *J. Mark.* **2010,** *74* (1), 65–79.

Fullerton, G. When Does Commitment Lead to Loyalty? *J. Serv. Res.* **2003,** *5* (4), 333–344.

Greene, W. E.; Walls, G. D.; Schrest, L. J. Internal Marketing: The Key to External Marketing Success. *J. Serv. Mark.* **1994,** *8* (4), 5–13.

Gronroos, C. *Internal Marketing Theory and Practice*, America Marketing Association's Services Conference Proceeding; 1985, pp 41–47.

Gummeson, E. Marketing Orientation Revisited: The Crucial Role of Part- Time Marketer. *Eur. J. Mark.* **1991,** *25* (2), 60–75.

Herrington, G.; Lomax, W. *Do Satisfied Employees Make Customers Satisfied? An Investigation into the Relationship Between Service Employee Job Satisfaction and Customer Perceived Service Quality*, Proceeding of the 28th EMAC Conference, Humboldt University, Berlin, May 11–14, 1999; pp. 110–117.

Joe, B. *The Antecedents and Consequences of Organizational Commitment: The Roles of Organizational Learning Culture, Leader-Member Exchange Quality, and Turnover Intention*, Midwest Academy of Management Conference, 2008.

Kukreja J. Lean Organizations Lead with Internal Marketing. *Asia Pacific J. Manag.* **2019a,** *1* (CII), 7–12.

Kukreja, J. Internal Marketing: Growth Fuel for Leading Organizations. *HRM Rev.* **2019b,** *15* (6), 25–30.

Lings, I.; Greenley, G. E. Measuring Internal Market Orientation. *J. Serv. Res.* **2005,** *7* (3), 290–305.

Malhotra, N.; Mukherjee, A. Analyzing the Commitment-Service Quality Relationship: A Comparative Study of Retail Banking Call Centre and Branches. *J. Mark. Manag.* **2003,** *19* (9), 941 971.

Mowday, R. T.; Steers, R.; Porter, L. W. *Organizational Linkages: The Psychology of Commitment, Absenteeism and Turnover*; Academic Press: Santiago, CA, 1982.

CHAPTER 10

Fintech: Disruption in International Education Sector

AMIT KUMAR SINGH, HARSHITA GUPTA, and
ROHIT KUMAR SRIVASTAV

Department of Commerce, Delhi School of Economics, Delhi University, New Delhi, India

ABSTRACT

Fintech, being a financial technology, is a disruption in traditional services and provides solutions for financial services and nonbanking finance services. It is a new concept in the financial sector and buzzword in today's world. The main objective of the present study is to assess opportunities and challenges in the Fintech sector. It explains how the evolution of the Fintech industry happened and presents Fintech in the finance sector. Fintech generates a digital transfer of money which is safe for every user. Fintech services are going at faster rates in the world. However, the speed of its growth could be maximized if certain hurdles in the path of fintechs are reduced.

10.1 INTRODUCTION

Fintech short for financial technology had a modest beginning in the 20th century when it was used as a back-end system of established institutions. However, today the concept has taken a 360° turn by becoming the most

Revolutionary Challenges and Opportunities of Fintech. Shweta Anand, PhD, Shalini Srivastav, PhD, Vikas Garg, PhD, & Geetika Garg (Eds.)

sought-after technology revolutionizing the entire financial landscape. Anything and everything which uses technology in conducting business can be called as Fintech.

Applications are wide ranging from simple money transfers to transacting in cryptocurrencies, industry applications ranging from a small departmental store to the most complex investment bankers. Need and innovation dynamics have led to the almost universal application of Fintech to even the smallest and untouched areas across the globe.

Global adoption rates of Fintech from 16% in 2016 to 64% in 2019 (Global Fintech adoption report 2019, EY) clearly show that it is much more than merely a hype. The ever-increasing applications are anything but beyond expectations when it began with Fedwire (1918), the first electronic fund transfer system (Ross et al., 2016). According to EY's report on global Fintech adoption 2019, Fintech has become the norm that governs the entire landscape of how we transact. The reports show that the estimated size of global Fintech industry at $128 Billion in 2018 is set to grow at nearly 25% per annum to $310 Billion in 2022 with newer geographies marking a higher share in the coming years. Currently, the Asia Pacific region commands the highest share in the Fintech revolution with China and India in the lead.

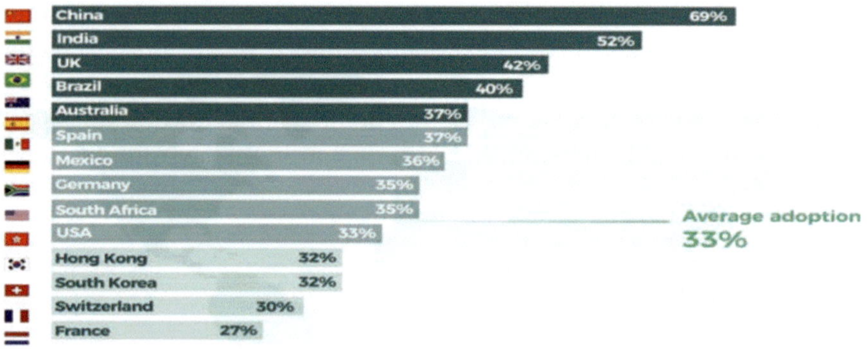

FIGURE 10.1 Regional Fintech adoption.

Image credit: EY global adoption index 2019

Several recent studies have focused on the reasons that made Fintech so successful with most of them concluding the benefits that this technology-led revolution provided at both ends of the conundrum (Doganova and Eyquem-Renault, 2009). On one hand, the consumers were able to fulfill the ever greater need of a simpler, innovative, tech-friendly, and convenient system. Generation Z knows no delay and wants everything on a tap of their finger. More adult population looked for time-saving, reliable, and reputed way of dealing with day-to-day activities (Osterwalder and Pigneur, 2010). On the other side, companies with young entrepreneurs taking charge knew no barrier when it comes to exploiting the market potential of any new idea. Even more, experienced and successful business houses all over the world realized that when you cannot beat it, you must partner it (FRBSF, 2012). The magnificent push for digitization by governments of major Asian countries and regulations become more business-friendly. Mobile-led Internet revolution has led to make Fintech the way of life for our upcoming generations (Park and Choi, 2016).

The Fintech ecosystem worldwide comprises various verticals in which Fintech has proved its mark such as Regulatory Technology (RegTech), Insurance Technology(InsureTech), Robo Advisors, Personal Finance, Alternative Finance, Payments and Remittances Blockchain and bitcoins, Digital Banks, etc. In the rest of the sections, we will discuss the revolutionary impact that Fintech has created in the education sector which is now popularly called EdTech (Jutla and Sundararajan, 2016).

10.2 UNDERSTANDING FINTECH

The term Fintech indicates products and processes that are made available for financial services globally (Vijai, 2019). As per the Financial Stability Board, Fintech is defined as "financial innovation made possible by technology that has a meaningful impact on financial markets, institutions, and the provision of financial services." It includes new business models, apps, processes, or products. As cited in the study of Vijai (2019) that as per Dorfleitner et al. (2017), FinTech can be categorized into broadly four segments namely Asset Management, Payments, Financing and Other FinTech. Figure 10.2 defines this structure.

10.2.1 BACKGROUND OF FINTECH

Fintech is considered a relatively an innovative and new term but the process of this has been around for a while. Gradually, it has become into a huge Fintech industry across the world that comprises of the both startups and renowned financial establishments endeavoring to improve the financial services-related administrations provided by financial organizations across the globe (McAuley, 2015). As early as the 1900s, organizations all over the world have endeavored to utilize constantly evolving technology to create present-day techniques for dealing with cash. A considerable lot of us may not understand; however, innovation has constantly assumed a noteworthy job in the money-related part. Moreover, the past 65 years clearly critical in the advancement of the Fintech industry and the development of a few Fintech arrangements (Enkel et al, 2009).

The 1950s saw the introduction of credit cards and 10 years later ATMs revolutionized how money was withdrawn from banks. Notwithstanding, it was distinctly with the approach of the advanced Internet during the 1990s, the Fintech business gotten move on quickly changed the situation with Fintech arrangements like electronic payment system, e-commerce business models, mobile banking, online-based shopping, and digitization of banks (Bhattacharya and Thakor, 1993).

Barclays launched the first ATM in the world in 1967; NASDAQ pioneered electronic trading and the IPO in 1971; PayPal launched its first online payment system in 1998; the first Bitcoin was launched in 2009; Google launched its Google Wallet in 2011, and the first Fintech bachelor was founded in 2016. These are some of the significant technological developments that have paved the way for the Fintech revolution. Financial innovation is said to be a disruptive force that previously and future are relied upon to reshape the financial-related part, plans of action, and banking structures. There is no uncertainty that the change came in with loads of skepticism, yet it was in the end acknowledged (Chesbrough, 2007). The ongoing development of the new financial technology innovation has attracted financial experts from all over, paving the door for emerging markets, and a thriving Fintech sector. Retail banking, payments and fund transfers, brokerage services, insurance, investments and wealth management, and commercial banking are among the many areas of the financial sector that are most impacted by the growth of Fintech (Bhandari, 2016).

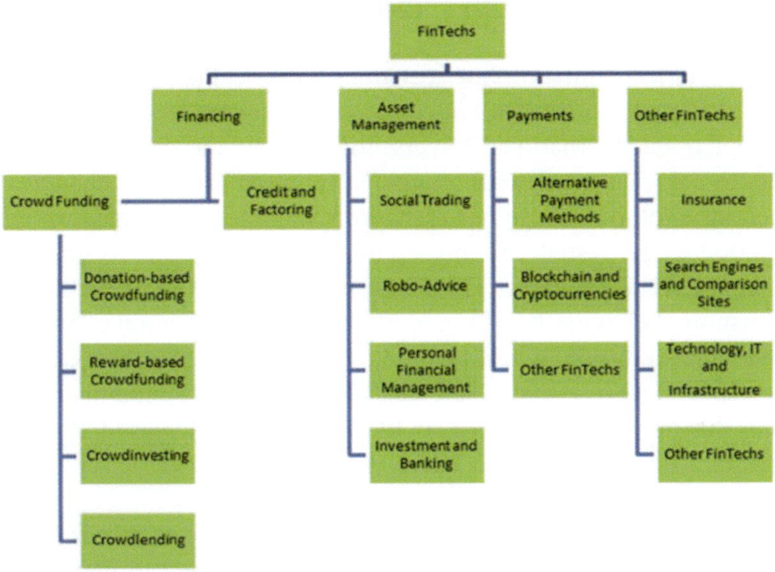

FIGURE 10.2 Categories of fintechs.
Source: Reprinted with permission from Dorfleitner et al., 2017). © Springer.

TABLE 10.1 Evolution of Fintech Industry.

1860	Invention of the pantelegraph
1880	Consumption of charge plates and charge coins on credit
1918	Fedwire invented
1919	An important book was introduced connecting finance and technology
1950	Credit card introduced by Diners Club
1958	Credit card was marketed by American Express
960	Stock market quotes were started displaying by Quotron
1966	Telex Network replaced by telegraph
1967	Barclays bank installed the first ATM
1971	NASDAQ established
1982–1983	Starting of online trade and banking
2009	Introduction of Bitcoin
2011	Google wallet introduced Google pay and send mechanism
2017	Alibaba introduced service of smile to pay

Source: www.getsmarter.com.

10.3 THE FINTECH ECOSYSTEM

Startups offering digital mobile recharges have occupied a prominent role in kick-starting expansion of Fintech globally. For an extremely prolonged stretch of time, international buyers utilized coupons bought from retail outlets to a great extent with money for prepaid mobile recharges. This created an evolution to digital recharge which actually transformed this into digital wallet system and infused the use of digital wallets for different other commercial activities. These new offerings also had a big impact on the consumer behavior. It has not only attracted the attention of tech-savvy people but also infused a vast amount of investments too. An examination of the eco-system of Fintech start-ups, particularly those found after 2007, depicts that capital investment in these start-ups increased to USD 25 million in 2013, in 2014 USD 109.1 million, and in 2015 it reported total investments of USD 364.6 million.

Remarkably, capital investment in Fintech start-ups is not restricted to digital wallets. The numbers of starts are considered to increase more in the future keeping in view of the different types of programs that are being run by the local or regional government in order to increase the pact of growth related to baking sector. This is further observing support from prominent corporations and VCs. Segment-focused VC firms have just tried to capture the first layer cream out of the potentials of this FinTech. It is just opposite to the developed markets like the USA where Fintech-focused VC companies (like QED Investors, Nyca Partners, and Ribbit Capital) can be found. Though, the lack of segment-focused VC firms does not indicate that there will be shortfall in the investment with reference to Fintech startups.

10.4 DIFFERENT FINTECH THEMES

Fintech has emerged as an economic agent that is not only helping the start-up ecosystem to grow. The recent emergence in Fintech companies globally has opened up new doors for payments, personal finance, lending, and other economic avenues. It is allowing the entire value chain system of old-style fiscal institutions in order to begin improved connections with consumers and providing new contributions in market internationally. There are different types of themes with regard to Fintech that is identified in the present scenario.

10.4.1 NEXT-GENERATION PAYMENTS

It is believed that next-generation payment systems are going to be driven by FinTech. As per KPMG Report (2016), 46% of Indian FinTech are focusing on trade and payment processing activities. Recently, UPI initiatives are expected to draw a new line of the future.

10.4.2 PEER-TO-PEER (P2P) LENDING

Peer-to-peer (P2P) which is also familiarized with P2P lending is creating a new platform to lend money to either businesses or individuals by removing the middleman. This P2P is entering into the regulatory paradigm and the numbers of P2P lending FinTech are growing year by year. This is not only helping the money deficit units to get the money but also contributes a bit to the growth of the economy.

10.4.3 BANK IN A BOX

In its initial days, the bank-in-a-box arrangement was primarily deployed by nonbanking financial institutions that needed to change from a lending-only model to a deposit-taking firm. Indeed, even up to this point, it was viewed as a decent alternative for little banks that did not have the ability to ace the intricacy of coordinating different technologies and solutions. In any case, new financial organizations and expanding rivalry, customer expectations, and administrative prerequisites have pushed banks to enter the market rapidly with the correct customer solutions. Accordingly, huge banks are additionally receiving the model and working with strategic partners to hold a sharp spotlight on their core business.

This is an integrated solution that has the change in core banking activities utilizing a specialist organization or the interface related to third party. It is adaptable and financially savvy and incorporates web besides versatile investment, store and credit items, ATM and POS switching, payment solutions, MIS reporting and regulatory. The product can undoubtedly be utilized by those people who are not even IT-specialists and are developing the new Fintech products to tapping more. The suite goes about as a total innovation arrangement crossing over the different delivery channel, among reconciliation and settlement and front-and back-office.

Although with the evolution of RRBs and payment banks has created a surge in the demand but this Fintech theme is going to create a disruption in the traditional playing field.

10.5 FINANCIAL INCLUSION

Financial inclusion is tool that is being rapidly used by many economies nowadays. Basically, it gives access to businesses and individuals to affordable and useful financial services and products which encounter their needs with regard to expenses, transactions, credit, savings, and assurance that is going to be delivered in a more supportable and accountable way, regardless of their personal wealth (Zilahy, 2016). Even having a bank account is the first phase toward achieving a wider goal of financial inclusion as having access to an account allows us to send and receive money along with storing it. A bank account works as a doorway to further different financial facilities that a person may need for personal as well as professional purposes. Even the World Bank Group's initiative of "Universal Financial Access 2020" focuses on advocating on providing the use of a bank account to every citizen of a nation so that the basic financial services could be accessed by the person.

The access to financial facilities not only facilitates people in their day-to-day activities but also helps the different businesses and families internationally for planning related to long-term horizon and unexpected crises as well. Being the accountholders, the individuals are further expected to use different types of financial facilities like insurance and credit in order to start and also to expand businesses, manage risk, invest in health or education, and other financial jolts that may progress the overall quality of their lives.

It has been seen that in 2013, working-age people around 2 billion did not have access to financial services globally. In Sub-Saharan Africa, for example, only 24% of adults are reported to have a bank account although in Sub-Saharan Africa, the financial sector has grown in the recent years.

Although there is always some degree of skepticism among the experts, regarding the effectiveness of different types of initiatives that have been taken under the umbrella of financial inclusion. Research on microfinance initiatives indicates that the wide availability of credit for microentrepreneurs can produce informal intermediation, an unintended form of entrepreneurship.

Fintech is storming in just because a lot of governments led initiatives are being taken throughout the country in order to adopt holistic measure to cover more number of people in the spectrum of financial inclusion.

10.5.1 BLOCKCHAIN

Basically, blockchain is literally only a chain of blocks but in the traditional way as per the words, the word block refers to digital information that is stored in a chain that is a public database. It has specifically three parts. First of all, it stores information about transactions buying goods, date, time, currency, etc. Secondly, the block store information related to the participants that are involved in these transactions. Lastly, blocks store the information in such a way that distinguishes them from each other. Each block assigns a unique code to information which is known as a hash which allows differentiating every block. A single block can store up to 1 MB of data, meaning that it can store a few thousand transactions.

No industry shall be so much benefitting from the blockchain by integrating it into the business as much as the banking industry. Basically, the financial institutions work within a fixed working week. So, if somebody needs to operate his/her account through a bank or deposit a cheque in the bank just a day before weekend then it may be quite possible that cheque is likely to get cleared on Monday or Tuesday of the coming week. Sometimes due to technical problems, it may get delayed even more due to the verification process and a large size of volume of transactions that a financial institution needs to operate. But with the introduction of blockchain, this time lag can be reduced as it is said that blockchain never sleeps (Agarwal and Hauswald, 2010).

10.5.2 ROBO-ADVISORY

Robo-advisors are basically a kind of digital platform that provides automated and algorithm-determined services in the context of fiscal planning by nominal or almost no human intervention. Generally, this Fintech, first of all, collects the information from all the clients with respect to their current economic scenario and enquires about the forthcoming aims of the clients with the help of survey through online and then it uses data in order to provide automated assistance and invest client's money. Nowadays, robo-advisors are offering easy account setup, portfolio management, security features, account services, robust goal planning, and attentive customer service at a very low fee. Although its coverage is very small in size but it can change a whole lot of games with regard to individual personal financial management. There is a need to undertake new and innovative ways to make this robo-advisory Fintech in tune to the current needs of the individuals.

10.5.3 SECURITY AND BIOMETRICS

Gone are the days when we used to operate our accounts physically by visiting the bank branches. Now, if anyone wants to pay for some services or transfer money to somebody's accounts, this is actually made possible by the digital intervention. This digital intervention has increased the transactions speed along with providing the opportunity to account holders to do other different activities along with sending money online or even paying the bills through the account.

With respect to Edu Techs, now the learners can use this Fintech in order to learn the new skills, understand theories; get aware about the different concepts related to their study even without visiting any institution for the same. All one need to do is to access that service online. These Edu Techs have enabled the students to go along with learning path without having any kind of disruption worldwide. So, this disruption in the traditional mode of study has opened a variety of new dimensions of learning (Viacom Media Networks, 2013).

But with rapid increase in the usage of this FinTech, there is a concern for security too. As per the recent regard, the security and biometrics-related Fintech are increasing a lot. Later on, we could see biometric security being utilized broadly all through the money-related assistance industry. Biometric security includes utilizing a person's biological qualities to recognize them, for instance unique mark or iris acknowledgment. This innovation could be profoundly useful for the money-related help industry since it is more secure than a secret key or PIN code and it could likewise conceivably reduce expenses by decreasing the requirement for two-advance confirmation by means of the SMS message.

Numerous monetary specialist organizations despite everything depend upon nonexclusive passwords, for example, mother's last name by birth and spot of birth. The entirety of this individual data is effectively accessible via web-based networking media. A few banks are as of now moving ceaselessly from this kind of secret word and rather utilizing one-time just passwords that are sent straightforwardly to the client's telephone each time they need to get to their bank or advance supplier. The development of one-time passwords is a positive advance to improving security, yet it will set aside a long effort to completely actualize them over all the money-related assistance segments. Some smart promoting procedures will likewise be required to get clients ready for the procedure.

As innovation improves and persistently develops, security turns out to be progressively significant. While new innovations are being utilized in organizations and administrations are commonly a positive, it can likewise leave them powerless against the most recent cybercrime, for example, hacking and data fraud (Dahlander and Gann, 2010). Voice recognition systems are gaining momentum in the recent economic scenario.

10.6 REVOLUTION IN EDUCATION THROUGH TECHNOLOGY—EDTECH

10.6.1 OVERVIEW

Traditionally education in almost all parts of the world has been restricted to classroom interaction between teacher–students with learning imparted using chalk and duster. Fintech, an integral component of the Fourth Industrial Revolution with pinch of technology and a touch of innovation, has forced us to mend our traditional ways of how we looked at our education sector. From schools in the box in Africa to e-learning, alternate financial tools for education we have come a long way.

10.7 VENTURE CAPITALISM AND EDUCATION SECTOR

The education industry is huge, and huge means $5 trillion globally per annum. For the time immemorial education has got a sacred importance in terms of upliftment of human race from the shadows of ignorance to illuminating us to go on the right path. However, a very little emphasis was being given to the market potential of this ever-booming industry with only 2% digitization till 2016 but that is no longer the case now. With each passing year billions of investments flowing into the education sector, it has taken a center stage with huge growth potential. The level of investment in learning solutions companies reached $19 billion globally in 2019 and the whole industry is projected to grow at 17% p.a. to $252 Billion in 2020 (Source: Financial Digest).

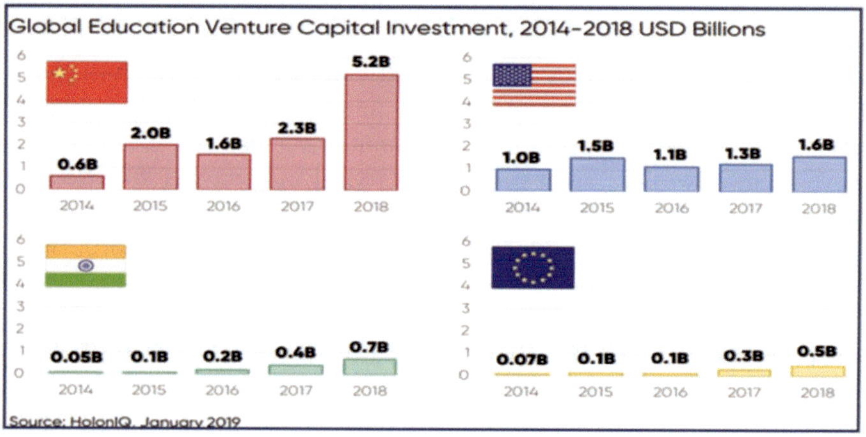

FIGURE 10.3 Investment in the Fintech-based education Sector over 2014–2018 in China, India, USA, and Europe.

Source: HolonIQ January Report, 2019

Venture capitalists are increasingly investing in digitization of the learning process in schools, developing cognitive, AI and artificial reality (AR) learning-based solutions. Mobile learning with interactive apps, location-based learning facilities, game learning theories, and even the advent of educational Bots such as Botsify which answers student's queries, teaches chapters, etc., platforms such as Course Q provide an interactive platform for students to virtually submit assignments and broadcast questions have taken it to an altogether different level. According to Crunchbase database EdTech companies such as Guorou (China) and Course hero (US) have raise nearly $14 and $27 million, respectively.

With majority of funding directed toward K-12 education and learning solutions 14 unicorns have built up globally namely Byju's (India) in July

2019, Coursera (USA) in April 2019, VIP kid (China) in September 2019, etc. Due to the abundance of capital chasing innovative solutions nearly 4000 EdTech companies have sprung up worldwide. The growing interests of venture capitalists also signify the future potential that this sector holds.

Financial sector known for its keen attention to profitable opportunities is partnering with educational institutes as knowledge partner to build a mutually beneficial partnership. The services on offer majorly include app-based subscriptions, access to their payment mechanisms, installation of newer technologies, preparing students for next-level challenges through updated courses and sessions, creating virtually simulating environment in lieu of payment, etc. Additionally, finance companies all over the world are also partnering with premier educational institutes for better Fintech ideas through their entrepreneurship cells that can be tested on their platforms and made available for a wider audience on maturity.

10.8 STUDENTS AND THE FINTECH REVOLUTION

Students across the world have been spoilt for choices with thousands of firms focusing on providing student-centric solutions to their real problems. Today, we can find an app on pretty much everything. The ever-expanding EdTech landscape includes the following.

- Immersive Tech: It is the use of AR, virtual reality (VR), and machine learning technology in learning. Research suggests that nearly 87% of students are more likely to attend classes due to introduction of tech-friendly classes. When students are able to virtually access the content through a combination of cloud services via trained professionals, interactive e-learning classes in a fully gamified experience they are more likely to become smarter and better prepared. System algorithm makes the system more intelligent that enables performance tracking, personalization of learning. Lecture VR and Google Expeditions Pioneer program are some of the examples in this area.
- Early childhood learning: Specialized, personalized, interactive learning apps using gaming and play way approach have cropped up for development of 3–5 years old.
- Student loans: Refinancing of student loans, hostel expenses, international study-to-ensure finance is no barrier companies such as M power are empowering youth with easy and specialized financing options.

- Language Learning: Multi-Lingualism has become a necessity and subscription-based apps such a babble are becoming a child's best partner.
- Fees payments, overseas money transfer either to parents or to educational institutes: Advent of simpler, convenient, and user-friendly payment mechanism have facilitated reliable and timely payment of education expenses. Companies such as Paypal, Paytm, Razorpay, Onfees, etc., are best-suited examples. Also, the trend for instant credit for fee payment is becoming popular with FeEs being one such platform. France's Financial Business schools accept fees through cryptocurrency. International scholarships and lower interest rate loans have become a common practice.
- Increasing financial literacy: Mobile money and finance-based knowledge apps have led the world to better understand their basic finances and make informed decisions.
- MOOCs, online courses, learning management system, coding and technology, government exams preparations and add-on courses, robotics, and coding knowledge—all these platforms increase the learning appetite of students and they are enthralled to get into a program for 10–12 weeks and get qualified.
- Fintech education, STEM: science, engineering, technology, mathematics learning, skills upgrade, and better placements—technical knowledge is no longer an add-on but a prerequisite for a finance student. Singapore has taken the challenge heads on. It is developing a curriculum to transform itself into a Fintech hub of the world. Monetary Authority of Singapore already committed to infuse around US$167 million for providing support in order to reach this goal over a period of 5 years.
- Social-emotional learning: student emotional and mental wellbeing. Stimulating environments generate a reaction from its receivers which can be analyzed to better predict and understand human learning behavior.

10.9 ISSUES AFFECTING FINTECH

Some of these factors are discussed below:

- Low penetration of Internet: In order to expand the Fintech sector, we need good Internet connectivity in terms of users. Developing nations do not have a good population that is connected with Internet or having a smartphone or similar time of electronic gadgets. Therefore, population that are accessing the Internet is low in numbers.

- Problem of bank accounts: Even if many steps are being taken under financial inclusion by governments from time to time to deliver basic financial facilities, especially the people that are living in different rural areas. Even after so much of this, large population that are living in villages do not have their personal bank accounts. This creates it harder for Fintech to produce, particularly in rural areas.
- Absence of technological infrastructure: Although countries have come a long way in the matter of developing technological infrastructure but still if we look at the growth rate in the creation and set-up of new hardware and technologies to support Fintech, we are still having miles to go. This problem is becoming hurdle for not only users of Fintech services but also the entrepreneurs that are aspiring to create a new Fintech start-up.
- Lack of Funds: It is very much clear that without the funds no organization could live and survive. What is happening with the fate of Fintech is that they are generally having a small organization in the beginning and therefore they have to rely on the private equity in order to survive and grow. It is not an easy task in for these new entrants in Fintech world to get the ample support from the financial institutions to get the funds for starting and running a Fintech institution. So, due to lack of availability of funds, even the good opportunities in the Fintech world are missed.
- Regulatory hurdles: Being a relatively new phenomenon, Fintech has aggressively established its footprints across segments; however, governments due to their very nature have seen it through a conservative lens. Governments are strongly heading toward regulations but it is too early for clarity on this front that hurts the development of this sector. Also, the risk of under-representation too poses a problem we are yet to deal with.
- Transaction costs: EdTech is still at a very nascent stage and hence due to huge costs of innovation, lack of economies of scale, infrastructural requirements and training costs, etc., make it costly for large-scale implementation especially in low-income countries.

- System inadequacy: The tools and arrangements that we have used for so long have started becoming obsolete and EdTech is here to change everything for the better.
- Awareness and comfort with technology: Traditional system of education has long served our definition of education and hence a change is difficult to absorb. It will take some time before we establish a similar level of comfort and create adequate system compatibility with the technology.
- Innovation and risk: The sector is largely untapped and offers abundant opportunities for growth and profitability. While the good times seem merrier but we must exercise caution about the things that may go wrong.
- See saw between public and private: Markets can be a powerful avenue to raise investments and solve the majority of innovators problems. But this area requires very sensitive analysis as the stakeholders is the society. Conflicting interests may ruin the sector potential and thus interests of public and private investors must align.
- The heavy skewedness of market to a select counties such as China, India, and the USA can impact the solutions being created globally. The westernized version of everything is considerably different from the rest of the world. With multinational corporations expanding their presence a polycentric approach is desirable.
- Companies will have to work harder for developing the trust and making the world of online financing more secure, transparent, and affordable. Though the mobile revolution has widened the accessibility and scope of the system manifold but still constraints such as low Internet connectivity, uneasiness while using the system, lack of training and awareness have held back the revolution from fully blossoming.

10.10 CONCLUSIONS

Any education system must be developed to encourage and support learners. EdTech is all about leveraging the benefits of technology to enable effective learning and increase the quality of our education system.

Done properly this can create a truly interactive and fruitful experience for our students.

Broad categories of change include:

- Personalizing the learning experience.
- Opening up the world of Internet and complementing the traditional learning processes.
- Equipping teachers with the right tools to generate results.
- Supporting global education and collaborative learning.
- Easing the access to financial resources, etc.

Fintech has truly disrupted the world of education; however, still the condition today is grim with most of the population across globe lacking the skills they need for a respectable standard of living. It will take years for us to fill the gap at this pace. Technology is the only ray of hope that can help us count leaps and move to a brighter future.

KEYWORDS

- **transaction cost**
- **global education**
- **collaborative learning**
- **emotional intelligence**
- **immersive technology**

REFERENCES

Agarwal, S.; Hauswald, R. Distance and Private Information in Lending. *Rev. Financ. Stud.* **2010,** *23* (7), 2757–2788.

Arner, D. W.; Barberis, J. N.; Buckley, R. P. The Evolution of Fintech: A New Post-Crisis Paradigm? 2015. SSRN 2676553.

Bhandari, M. India and the Pyramid of Opportunity. The Fintech Book: The Financial Technology Handbook for Investors, Entrepreneurs and Visionaries **2016,** *1*, 81–83.

Bhattacharya, S.; Thakor, A. V. Contemporary Banking Theory. *J. Financ. Intermed.* **1993,** *3* (1), 2–50.

Chesbrough, H. W. Business Model Innovation: It's Not Just About Technology Anymore. *Strategy Leadership* **2007,** *35* (6), 12–17.

Dahlander, L.; Gann, D. M. How Open Is Innovation? *Res. Policy* **2010,** *39* (6), 699–709.

Desai, F. The Fintech Boom and Bank Innovation. Forbes, 2015. https://www.forbes.com/sites/falgunidesai/2015/12/14/t he -Fintech-revolu-tion/#1202f56249d0

Doganova, L.; Eyquem-Renault, M. What Do Business Models Do? Innovation Devices in Technology Entrepreneurship. *Res. Policy* **2009,** *38* (10), 1559–1570.

Dorfleitner, G.; Hornuf, L.; Schmitt, M.; Weber, M. *Fintech in Germany*; Springer Nature, 2017.

Enkel, E.; Gassmann, O.; Chesbrough, H. Open R&D and Open Innovation: Exploring the Phenomenon. *R&D Manage.* **2009,** *39* (4), 311–316.

Federal Reserve Bank of San Fransisco (FRBSF). Is the Fed Still in the Business of Processing Checks? 2012. http://www.frbsf.org/education/publica¬tions/doctor-econ/2012/april/check-processing

Fintech in India. A Report Published by Swissnex India, Consulate General of Switzerland, 2016.

Jutla, S.; Sundararajan, N. India's Fintech Ecosystem. In The Fintech Book: The Financial Technology Handbook for Investors; Entrepreneurs and Visionaries, 2016; pp 56–57.

Kandpal, V.; Mehrotra, R. (2019). Financial Inclusion: The Role of Fintech and Digital Financial Services in India. *Indian J. Econ. Busi* **2019,** *19* (1), 85–93.

KPMG. Fintech in India: A Global Growth Story. Joint Publication by KPMG in India and NASSCOM 10,000 Startups, 2016.

McAuley, D. What Is Fintech? Wharton FinTech, 2015.

McKinsey & Company. Cutting Through the Fintech Noise: Markers of Success, Imperatives For Banks; McKinsey & Company, 2015.

Osterwalder, A.; Pigneur, Y. *Business Model Generation: A Handbook for Visionaries, Game Changers, and Challengers*; John Wiley & Sons: New York, 2010

Park, Y.; Choi, J. The Adoptionof Mobile Payment Services for "Fintech". *Int. J. Appl. Eng. Res.* **2016,** *11* (2), 1058–1061.

The Pulse of Fintech survey, KPMG, February, 2016.

Viacom Media Networks. *The Millennial Disruption Index*; Viacom, 2013

Vijai, C. Fintech in India-Opportunities and Challenges. SAARJ J. Bank. Insurance Res. (SJBIR) **2019,** *8* (1), 42–54.

Zilahy, G. Sustainable Business Models—What Do Management Theories Say? *Vezetéstudomány/Budapest Manage. Rev.* **2016,** *47* (10), 62–72.

CHAPTER 11

Global Revolutionary Challenges and Opportunities of Fintech Globally

ANITA VENAIK, NISHTHA GARG, and VRINDA AGARWAL

Amity University, Noida Campus, Noida, Uttar Pradesh, India

ABSTRACT

Fintech is a common abbreviation for the term financial technology, which in today's modern era is considered as one of the trendiest fields to work for. It is mostly due to the very fact that financial technology has the future to transform and lead to enormous changes within the way of living of individuals along with how they run business globally. Fintech is essentially mentioned as a wide term that is basically used to categorize those organizations and start-ups which typically use cloud-based tools and various other sorts of technology so as to bring about an enhancement in the area of banking and finance. This field has taken into account sufficient prospective to bring in a revival of the present finance set-up, this is the reason why many regulators across the world have been working to hit a balance between innovation and protection. Types of innovations that seek to make financial resources more available to the general population include the use of smartphones for mobile banking, savings, crowdfunding services, and cryptocurrencies.

11.1 INTRODUCTION

The chief reason for Fintech globally to evolve was the gigantic amounts of money that was being flown within the financial system within the past

Revolutionary Challenges and Opportunities of Fintech. Shweta Anand, PhD, Shalini Srivastav, PhD, Vikas Garg, PhD, & Geetika Garg (Eds.)

few years. Buying capacity of an individuals and disposable cash was raising manifold that enabled venture funding and capital investments to grow significantly at an identical time worldwide.

However, it is still a growing industry, Fintech investments worldwide rose to $55.3 billion in 2018, more than double of the $26.7 billion in 2017. The Fintech field involves insurance technology (insurtech), regulatory technology (RegTech), financial data API's and mobile banking, along with other sorts of technology. Each represents a definite category of financial-specific technology.

The usage of the web along with the mobile Internet has brought a quick evolution in the field of finance technology across the world. In fact, slow moving, high regulated, and highly wary industry (such as insurance) have started adopting new innovative technology to improve the effectiveness and efficiency provided through Fintech solutions.

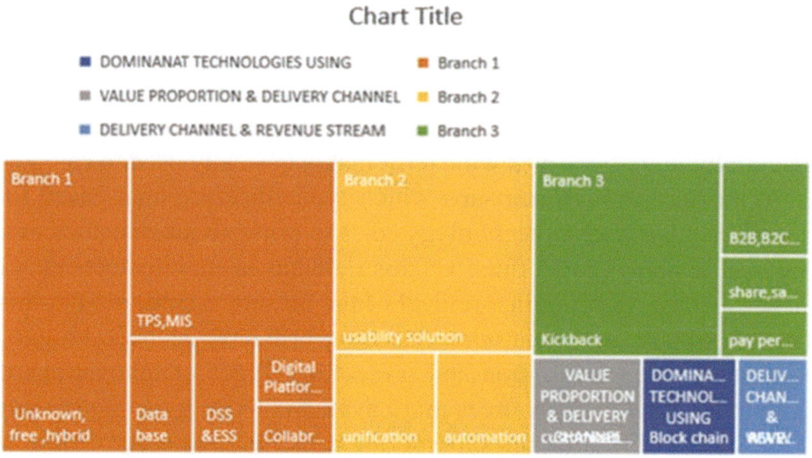

Business operation and business model of Fintech followed.

11.2 BENEFITS OF FINTECH

11.2.1 LOWER COST

Organizations most of the time gets benefit from innovative technology that gives higher automation of the process. Within the regulatory industry, financial institutes are focused to save large amount money by making use of reg-tech solutions. In addition to reducing on the employees required to perform jobs that might be automated, the insights obtained by applications of Fintech can help organizations to enhance operations effectiveness and efficiency.

11.2.2 IMPROVED DECISION MAKING

It is another area within which Fintech can extend help to organizations immensely, essentially with the increased use of AI. Organizations can now count upon insights driven by AI-powered and data-driven to develop strategies. With the availability of these insights, organizations might take better decisions about where to direct resources available and the way of focusing on individuals.

11.2.3 IMPROVED TRANSPARENCY

The most important benefit of Fintech, with special reference to AI-powered reg-tech for the finance sector and blockchain-based Fintech, is transparency introduction. Fintech-based projects generate testable financial trails and which might assist to spot possible fraudulent action quicker and in an easier way than an individual. The introduction of improved transparency, projects will bring about changes in the antimoney laundering and know your customer part of the sector internationally.

11.3 USES OF FINTECH

11.3.1 PAYMENTS

Moving cash all over is what Fintech is incredibly best at. The expression "I shall Venmo you" is now replacing "I shall pay you later." Venmo, for some obvious cause, is a common go-to mobile payment platform. Such payment firms have altered the process we all do our business. It is simple and easy to send money digitally anywhere within the globe.

11.3.2 LENDING

Fintech is additionally overhauling credit by smooth assessment of risk, accelerated process of approval, and enabling easier access. Many individuals all over the world could apply for a loan over a mobile phone, new information and finer risk modeling are enlarged credit to unworthy inhabitants. Also, individuals could ask for credit reports several times within a given year without clashing their score, enabling the complete back-end of the lending universe more transparent for everybody.

11.3.3 INSURANCE

With the passage of time, Insurtech is swiftly becoming its own industry; however, it comes under the umbrella of Fintech. Insurance is sort of unhurried adopter of innovative technology, and most of the Fintech start-ups have been establishing partnership with traditional insurance organizations to provide guidance about process automation and enlarge coverage. From having mobile insurance to wearables for health insurance, the industry is having a lot of innovation. Fintech innovations have affected the insurance sector by enhancing efficiency, reduced expenses, better assessment of risk, and offering smooth customer experience.

11.3.4 BANKING

Mobile banking constitutes a huge part of the Fintech industry. In the personal finance world, individuals have a high demand for simple digital access to their bank accounts, essentially on mobile phones. Many big financial institutions now give some kind of mobile banking options, owing to the increase of Neo banks. Neo banks have no physical branch locations, serving individuals by offering financial services completely on mobile phones.

11.3.5 REGTECH

RegTech (regulatory technology) aims at automation of compliance method for financing institutes. It provides with fast and cost-effective management of enormous amount of information, which includes records transactions and compliance information, like corporate tax returns.

11.3.6 APIS

Financing data APIs are mending the way the financing service sector view at banking and have strengthen the idea of open banking as a feasible idea. Open banking mention to banks that are opening up their large amounts of client's information which assist financing start-ups to evolve applications developed which assist banking users.

Data anonymization is the key to feasibility of open banking idea, it implies the information is clear of any personal data prior to being conferred. It enables the save guarding of individual privacy and helps organizations to make the use of this large database to evolve an innovative solution in the financing sector for the well-being of the whole sector. Regulators all over the world conduct the drive for open banking, generating legislation designed to stimulate competition, and user choice by introducing innovation within the industry.

Financial data APIs are multidimensional instruments that might be supported to give value in various ways, such as connecting businesses to stock information.

11.4 FINTECH KEY DRIVERS

11.4.1 CONSENT LAYER

The consent layer is used to provide consent for data exchange between two providers. It can be done with the help of "Digital Signature."

11.4.2 FAVORABLE GOVERNMENT INITIATIVES

Several initiatives launched by the Government of countries have given high hopes for populations of changing time. The initiatives made FinTech an essential component of daily commerce. It changes nations into digitally empowered societies and propels knowledge-based economies.

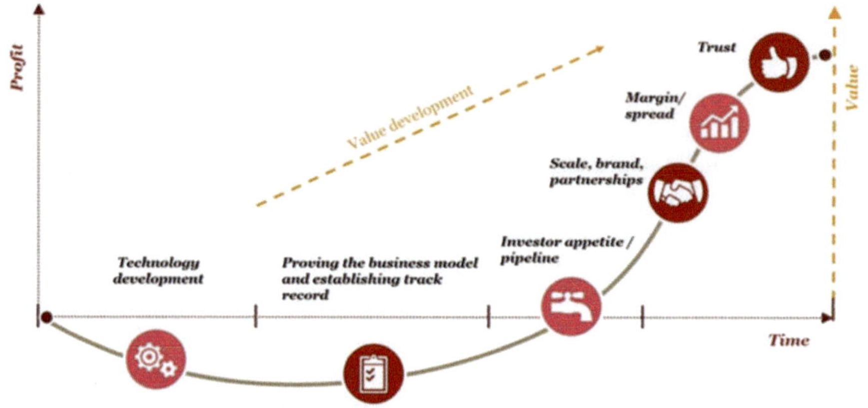

Various factors affecting growth of Fintech using time value proportion for growth.

11.4.3 BLOCKCHAIN

Blockchain is the major area of technology that is taking the Fintech revolution. It allows information to be distributed digitally but not copied. Blockchain uses an ingenious way of transferring information for say A to B in a safe manner. It works on distributed ledger technology that allows anyone to see everyone's entry and make it impossible for a single user to gain control. It ensures security, admin cost, and reduction in time (Bay, 2018).

ABI Research estimates that by 2023, the creation of blockchain applications will bring in more than $10.6 billion in revenue, primarily from investments in financial technology.

11.4.4 HIGH SMARTPHONE PENETRATION

Mass market penetration of smartphones has enabled internet access for variant people across the globe. Smartphones being the facilitator and primary means of internet access to most people provides very handy and secure access to digital banking via some third-party applications led to the highest Fintech adoption rate in any country.

11.4.5 NEW BUSINESS MODELS

Technology-driven business models such as the Internet of Things, machine learning, natural language processing, and artificial intelligence ensure the largest FinTech ecosystem globally.

11.5 OPPORTUNITIES & CHALLENGES OF FINTECH

11.5.1 OPPORTUNITIES

11.5.1.1 MICROFINANCING AND PEER-TO-PEER LENDING

Peer-to-peer lending organizations resolve a controversy that financial institutions often cannot resolve. They disintermediate the method of crediting, connecting prospective with borrowers' loan providers via P2P platforms (Lending Club, Prosper). Hence, it is easy to access consumer and business credits; the method becomes easy, efficient, and quick. The potential which lies in this prospect is yet to get unfolded.

A start-up named affirm combines the payment services along with lending services, offering an alternative finance tools. Namely, the product gives instalment payment offering their users to make payment for goods within a variety of online e-commerce platforms, which includes Eventbrite and Expedia.

So, lending industry is highly promising industry that is expected to achieve $1 trillion by the end of 2025.

Transparency as a unique selling point within the financial services industry.

The lack of transparency from traditional institutions on their services has led to customer distrust globally. Traditional large financing institutes have been constantly in search for excuses so as to maintain information hidden from its users, essentially if it is about the payment structure. Unsurprisingly, it particularly holds true within areas in which disclosure is not covered by regulation.

It gives opportunities for Fintech to penetrate into market gaps by generating trust by providing transparency. It works to provide encryption, to protect customer information, and allow clients to remove their personal data if they want to.

Customer relationships with traditional financial institutions no longer exist.

People divided the issues with today's financial system, such as giant banks, into three categories:

1. Consumers have a broken relationship with money; they are confused by the number of total accounts that are accessible and financial byproducts.
2. Borrowers are required to go through an uncomfortable process.
3. On the other hand, people who save sense disdain for the financial industry due to the minimal prospects of a return.

People now have a certain amount of mistrust for conventional banking institutions as a result.

This situation may be used by Fintech to create financial services that can actually meet the wants of customers.

For instance, a business strategy that depends on clients not paying back debts on time (thus causing late fees) (Lamest, 2018).

11.5.1.2 SMART WAY OF MANAGING PERSONAL FINANCE

Given the growth of Fintech, individuals are not required to have a degree in accounts to manage it. Various tools are available in market, which provide services like management of assets, planning finance required, etc.

Intuit Inc. is the undoubted commander in personal finance sector. Mint.com which is one of its unique products enables users to have a record of account, master cards, loans, and all other financial transactions, all through one application. Level Money is another application that enables users to connect with accounts with any 2500 available banks within the USA, allowing an easier way to manage accounts. Later, capital one took over the company. A representative of the company said, "one of various steps that company is taking to deliver is a new generation financial experience." This shows the trend of digitization among organizations.

However, there are still opportunities for better and smarter personal finance.

11.5.1.3 MAKING THE MOST OF BLOCKCHAIN MARKET

There are now too many firms entering the market with blockchain solutions, even if it is clear that the idea of decentralization will influence the future of financial services globally and the demand for blockchain experts is still rising. Given this growing trend, including the associated cryptocurrency in your portfolio of financial services (e.g., on a trading platform) could be a fruitful tactic for luring clients who, at a later stage, could be cross-sold a wider range of financial services. Indeed, eToro has benefited from adding cryptocurrency trading to their product range, suggesting that there is a robust demand for bitcoin trading chances.

Being aware of disruptive changes is, in general, the best strategy to prevent becoming one of the businesses that the ongoing changes.

11.5.1.4 INNOVATIVE WAY OF PROCESSING TRANSFER OF MONEY

Be it Stripe a system for mobile payment, Square a device that can process payments of credit card, or Transfer Wise which provides service to transfer money, any instrument which can fulfill the demand for fast, cheap, and convenient processing of payment has a huge potential. Additionally, Apple and Google wager on mobile payments, says it all.

11.5.1.5 EASIER WAY OF ACCOUNTING FOR SMALL GROUP OF BUSINESSES

To have a simple yet efficient and effective tool that can automate the management of personal financial is good. By making the use of paper and a pen or usage of Excel sheets to handle the financials of business is no more an option in times of digitization.

However, the uprising has just started: change to cloud SaaS technologies, financing is much more easy and secure. For instance, Wave gives tools focused to simplify finance for freelancers and small businesses, for free. By giving an alternative to big organizations, the company is providing a full set of accounting tools, from financing and invoicing to payroll payments and other services.

11.6 PREDICTIVE ANALYTICS AND BIG DATA

With the advancement of predictive analytics and Big Data, there has been an advancement of the financial sector. Goldman Sachs, Morgan Stanley, and various other financial institutes are currently in a hunt for innovative ways to make the use of information that they have collected over time.

Industry insights, gathered by making use of the innovative technologies, are what big organizations use to cope with the difficulties industry disruptors have been showing. Hence, their concern with big data and predictive analytics can be described easily (AltexSoft, 2016).

Citi Ventures, invested in a start-up named Feedzai, used to prevent fraud in e-commerce. In fact, prevention of fraud and risk management are a few noticeable areas of Fintech, where in machine learning along with data science has proved highly helpful.

11.7 CHALLENGES

11.7.1 LEGACY MODERNIZATION

Some systems are simply laborious to switch, for banks modernizing systems and frameworks is like getting an idea of how to back away from these decades-old legacy bank systems, on which their entire operations like account opening, setup, fund transfer, deposit processing, and loan processing rely.

11.7.1.1 WHAT IS LEGACY SYSTEM?

A legacy banking system is a set of older outdated software or historically grown system that is essential for day-to-day company operations and is in use by the employees but no longer meets the current needs. These are traditionally built a system that meets the very specific set of requirements but is not able to sustain and speed up the expansion to the new market.

In banks, legacy system is the inhibitors to technology disruption, as a result, many banks are delaying digital transformation and find it very challenging to replace legacy systems.

A few reasons why banks seem to be procrastinating the whole process of shifting from the old legacy system to modern technology are mainly due to the following:

- Rigid systems and the existing software are difficult to update. The whole process of change requires way too many resources, time investment, thought process, and multiple rounds of regression testing. Also, these types of projects and changes have a very high probability of failure.
- This evolution faces some internal and external challenges for bank like knowledge transfer, skills gap, undocumented logics, Fintech feeding all the information, and fast decision making. Failure of these projects led to damage of corporate and brand reputation as well as customer and shareholder's confidence.

Regardless of the rationale, fear and risk banks must move and need a well-formed strategic approach to switch obsolete systems over long term by launching several front-end customer apps working toward providing a good user experience to customers. They can dedicate an entire team of engineers, technicians to develop a whole new system to overtake the complete operations of the bank and business.

11.7.1.2 FINANCIAL ECOSYSTEM

Traditional banking systems, financial institution, and FinTech start-ups, nowadays, evolving from competition to collaboration. But it is not believed that FinTech will be able to replace legacy and traditional banks systems because consumers have decades of trust and relationship with bank. In this ecosystem, collaboration is the key to launch new products and services faster than before.

Financial institutions already started working with new ventures in numerous ways through mergers, partnerships, incubations, acquisition, mentoring programs, etc. Nevertheless, this is easier said than done, as both institutions run on their different well-defined different set of rules. In

India, we just cannot be left out tradition banking systems else these banks will soon become the Nokia of finance industry. Also, FinTech industry process requires patience and significant amount of time to gain immense trust of customers.

Now, there is the high time for both FinTech & traditional financial institutes to open up toward each other and explore their harmonies together. All components of financial ecosystem, that is, banks, and regulatory bodies require to perform as per the pace and disruption of technology and get benefitting by coming together in the market.

11.7.1.3 CYBER SECURITY

The nature of data hold by clients is very sensitive, and cyber-attacks are the greatest risk and challenge to all the business and concerned Fintech organizations Therefore, it is very vital to know the hidden cyber security risk associated with the adoption of FinTech.

11.8 DATA BREACHES AND DATA INTEGRITY

Data play a crucial role in every industry and when it comes to bank it becomes a matter of utmost importance.

Digitization led, people, use mobile phones more readily to access all their accounts information and made it very easy to transfer funds. The robust mobile applications provide banking customers with so much ease and quick workflows these apps tend to store all the payment card details and user information which become readily available to hackers making transactions prone to cyber thefts. All these financial institutions partners with third-party providers and then data loss and integrity risks occur due to their inefficient Fintech systems in the finance industry.

11.9 APPLICATION SECURITY RISK

Bank uses various mobile applications to provide access to real-time information to its customers. But if the application lacks vital security modules and efficient codes then the mobile application becomes prone to cyber-attack (Muhn, 2020).

11.10 ONLINE HACKING AND MALWARE ATTACKS

Online hacking and malware attacks are very prominent types of security issues. The majority of banks use SWIFT networks to exchange crucial financial information more securely. The recent breach on every single piece of SWIFT infrastructure, however, revealed the level of skill of the perpetrators. Because the banks and financial institutions' operations are vulnerable, hackers can use those weaknesses to launch virus assaults.

11.10.1 IS CRYPTOCURRENCY TECHNOLOGY SECURE?

Technology advancements have changed the way banks used to operate and with the exponential increase in cybercrimes, and in prevalent complaints of exploiting of sensitive information and personal data, users cannot stop wondering whether cryptocurrency is threat or not.

The only concern with the cryptocurrency transactions is that they are strenuous to trace which may provide a chance to hackers for manipulation of the systems and thus promotes means for various illicit activities and terrorism. However, this is not true.

Cryptocurrency works on blockchain technology. Blockchains allow all the transactions to be stored in a ledger, which is completely verified, thus sharing the information with all users to generate a secure, customary record. This distributed ledger technology has great potential to prevent currency reproduction, fraud, and double-spending. Cryptocurrencies act as a very serious competitor to the traditional banking systems, they are capturing a very big chunk of business relating to the transfer of money and payments. Banks are evolving themselves to embrace the technology as it might make intermediaries like banks redundant (Khandelwal, 2019).

11.11 4C'S TO WORK UPON

11.11.1 CREDIBILITY & CONSUMER CONFIDENCE

In FinTech industry, consumers are dealing with money; hence they are hesitant and not ready to show their faith toward Fintech innovation to streamline their daily monetary operations and financial decisions.

Consumers seem to be conservative and price sensitive. Providing financial services in an unbanked market becomes a challenge itself, due to lack of customer trust. People often relate these services with the digital scam, these people have very limited experience with the online world and transactions and are also not ready to accept the evolution of digital technology in financial services. Gaining their confidence, have them trust the FinTech product and services that are unfamiliar, takes a lot of time and effort.

11.12 CASH MARKET

In spite of demonization, India remains an exceedingly cash-intensive nation mainly because the lives of people are centered around being paid in cash and use cash for their purchases as well. It becomes very challenging for FinTech companies to gather information of customer and exchange of cash which are completely off-book.

11.13 CUSTOMER EXPERIENCE

Transforming the finance business is not at all a simple task. One of the largest barriers to build trust is to make sure the bank communicates and updates the clients regularly, despite any direct communications. FinTech corporations should be terse while not being boring, clear without eliminating crucial data, and transparent, however, not daunting to fulfill customer's desires.

If customers feel well and have a seamless experience on the website during purchasing process, they will return and frequently use it. It is always advisable to add the human element on websites by providing a number that customers can call for support if they encounter any kind of issue. For further lead generation, communication via social handles, email, and content marketing helps and allows customers to build the trust component. All these things brought by customer experience tend to be very important for FinTech business but at the same time giving a hard time to start-ups to make their space and brand by keeping their user expertise (UX) and computer program (UI) simple, online content original, relevant, interesting, and fascinating.

11.14 CUSTOMER RELATIONSHIPS

Customers do not like to switch their bank accounts. They do not want to take any risk and it is often difficult to convince them to try out your new solution FinTech companies need to understand their concern and provide the solution that fits their daily life ensuring long-term customer relationships. Forming a well-structured and compelling financial fitness program is challenging, but it helps to attract new customers and build much deeper relationships (Woepke, 2019).

11.15 LACK OF AWARENESS AND LIMITED UNDERSTANDING

Digitization buzz is among the urban people only, FinTech industry is lacking in providing clear guidelines to customers which led to the misconception that this industry is not secure like traditional financial institutions and preventing the industry to reach the rural population and its full potential.

To implement financial technology banks have to comply with regulatory standards to avoid facing legal penalties and paying hefty fees.

11.16 FINDING INVESTORS

FinTech start-ups require huge capital. Running a Fintech start-up is different from an average start-up due to its complex working model. Most of the FinTech offerings are service-based, therefore, arguably intangible. It is often difficult for start-ups to portray the value proposition to investors as more explanation and in-depth knowledge is required than in other industries unless they are pitching to technologically and financially savvy investors.

Moreover, traditional bank systems think of FinTech industry as rivals and this is the main reason that banks are hesitant to contribute and support these FinTech start-ups.

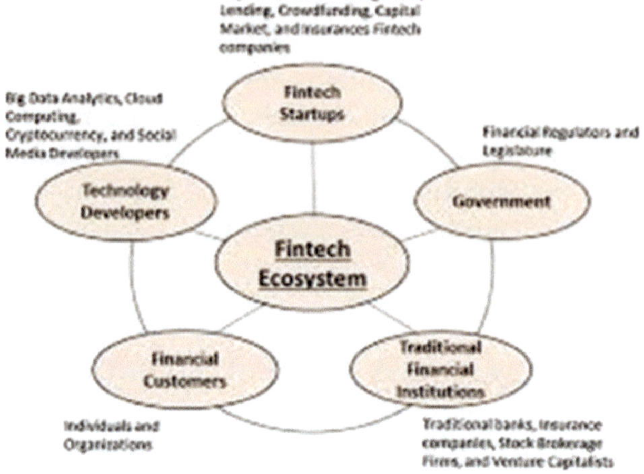

Source: Reprinted with permission from Lee et al. (2018). Copyright 2017 Kelley School of Business, Indiana University.

KEYWORDS

- **smartphones**
- **cryptocurrency**
- **Fintech**
- **technology**
- **business**

REFERENCES

AltexSoft. Unlocking Fintech Potential: Top 7 Opportunities to Transform Financial Industry with the Use of Technology, 2018. https://medium.com/@AltexSoft/unlocking-Fintech-potential-top-7-opportunities-to-transform-financial-industry-with-the-use-of-bbf11c48eb1c

Bay, O. Spurred by Digital Transformation and Smart Technologies, Blockchain Revenues to Hit US$10.6 Billion by 2023, 2018. https://www.abiresearch.com/press/spurred-digital-transformation-and-smart-technologies-blockchain-revenues-hit-us106-billion-2023/

Khandelwal, R. Are Cryptocurrencies and PayPal a Risk for Banking? 2019. https://marketrealist.com/2019/11/are-cryptocurrencies-and-paypal-a-risk-for-banking/

Lamest, M. Three Opportunities for Fintech Companies. Luxembourg Expert blog, 2018. https://blog.kpmg.lu/three-opportunities-for-Fintech-companies/?utm_source=Mondaq&utm_medium=syndication&utm_campaign=LinkedIn-integration

Lee, I., Shin, Y. J. Fintech: Ecosystem, business models, investment decisions, and challenges. Business horizons, (2018) 61(1), 35–46.

Muhn, J. Cybersecurity: The Hidden Risks of Fintech Services, 2020. https://finovate.com/cybersecurity-the-hidden-risks-of-Fintech-services/

Srikanth, R. P. How NPCI Became the Flag Bearer of India's Digital Revolution, 2017. https://www.expresscomputer.in/news/how-npci-became-the-flag-bearer-of-indias-digital-revolution/21276/

Szakiel, P. What Is Fintech: A Beginner's Guide to Financial Technology in 2019, 2018. https://learn.g2.com/Fintech

Woepke, S. The 4 Pillars of Successful Fintech-Customer Relationships, 2019. https://www.finance-monthly.com/2019/12/the-4-pillars-of-successful-Fintech-customer-relationships/

CHAPTER 12

Major Challenges and Benefits of Fintech Across the Globe

SHWETA ANAND[1], SHALINI SRIVASTAV[2], VIKAS GARG[3], and GEETIKA GARG[4]

[1]*School of Management, Gautam Buddha University, Greater Noida, India*

[2]*Amity University, Greater Noida Campus, Uttar Pradesh, India*

[3]*Amity University, Uttar Pradesh, India*

[4]*Bhai Gurdas Group of Institutions, Punjab, India*

ABSTRACT

Fintech, is short form of financial technology, aims to deliver financial services by making use of various software's through modern technology like internet, smartphone, cryptocurrency, etc. Fintech across the globe also includes sectors and industries such as education, retail banking, fund-raising, bitcoin, and investment management. The digital tools provided by Fintech are overpassing traditional business models with innovative ideas and various software solutions. Fintech is a platform where international customers will get opportunities to choose from number of large options at competitive/affordable prices and even financial Institutions can improve with low costs.

Revolutionary Challenges and Opportunities of Fintech. Shweta Anand, PhD, Shalini Srivastav, PhD, Vikas Garg, PhD, & Geetika Garg (Eds.)

12.1 INTRODUCTION

Fintech's demand across the globe is growing day by day due to big digitally savvy companies seeking new technologies, which provide convenience to use and better profitability. Fintech products help industries to attain cost efficiency and helping business grow fast. Some major benefits of Fintech are cost efficiency, improved decision making, and transparency. Fintech explores the potential of global market trends. There is a need of analysis of remaking of global trends in coming years and innovation on business models. Fintech products include Insurance Technology (Insuretech), API's, financial services, Mobile payment apps, regulatory trends (Regtech), and payments, etc.

Fintech is growing rapidly globally since the internet and smartphone revolution. The key takeaways of Fintech are to improve financial services and its delivery to consumers and Fintech funding is on rise in every country besides several regulatory issues. Till now financial services Institutions offered a lot of services under one roof. These services range from traditional banking facilities or services to trading services. Fintech enables the financial services companies to work efficiently and cutting down the cost associated with every transaction. New technologies like Artificial Intelligence (AI) and Data-driven marketing will learn the habits of customer's spending and saving and their decisions in a better way. The AI technology helps the customers with their works in an effective and speedy way and it keeps the staff cost low also.

Internationally Fintech users have four categories as Business customers, final consumers, B2B for financial services, and B2C for small-scale business. A lot of hurdles regarding taking loans, credit card payments (as they are landline-connected card readers) for collecting startup capital; are removed with mobile technology. This technology also brings certain problems also. All automation and digitalization process invites hackers who access the systems and steal all the information and misuse it. The other problem of Fintech is regulation especially in cryptocurrency. Initial coin offerings are used as a form of fundraising in which new firms raise money for capital directly from investors for their new businesses. Usually they are unregulated in various countries across the globe and it may lead to frauds and big scams. Respective governments of these countries are facing difficulties to formulate uniform regulations and norms to protect consumers because of variety of different types of services provided by Fintech. These governments are either using existing regulations or customizing the regulations according to the need and according to the financial culture in their countries.

12.2 PRESENT SCENARIO OF FINTECH GLOBALLY

According to EY Global Fintech Adoption Index; Fintech adoption rate in worldwide is 64% in 2019 in comparison to 16% in 2015 and 33% in 2017. This 64% adoption rate is 12% more than anticipated 52% in 2017's survey. China and India are ahead with 87% adoption rate followed by Russia and South Africa 82%, Netherland with 73%, UK and Ireland with 71%. According to report in Japan, France, and Chile, trust was the main factor in customers for not choosing a FinTech service over banks. Ninety-six percent of global consumers are aware of at least one money transfer and payment Fintech service. Only 4% out of total global consumers are not aware of any kind of money transfer and payment Fintech service.[1] India being a developing country is the fastest growing in Fintech and has been at forefront of Fintech Revolution. About alone 99.5% of respondents in countries of India and China are aware of mobile/online payment services and online money transfer, which is quite surprising figure being world's most populated countries.[3]

12.3 CHALLENGES AND OPPORTUNITIES OF FINTECH

Here are some challenges every Fintech will face in global context the journey from start-up to grown-up while offering their best.

12.3.1 REGULATORY LANDSCAPE

With the growing trends of Fintech globally there are many risks involved. These risks are associated with consumers, investors, and financial service firms worldwide and risks associated with financial stability. Risks to consumers include lack of consumer understanding, data privacy, security and protection, and mis-selling of Fintech products and services. Risks associated with firms include business model viability, technology risk, Governance, data handling, and legal issues. Risks associated with financial stability include risk of use of crypto assets, alternative channels, and herd-like behavior of investors. One of the main reasons of these risks is that the Fintech firms rely on technology using large sets of data. The second main reason is the complexity of Fintech sector and the third main reason is the herd-like behavior of planetary consumers because of same IT solutions.

The problem of regulation arises when the current regulations fail to cope with the changes in technology. Regulators across the globe are time to time reframing or redesigning parameters taking account of new or modified Fintech products and services. Fintech firms are also aware of the ways in which regulations affect their business. Fintech firms will be proactive so that they are able to think in advance about how they mitigate the risks associated with Fintechs. Regulators are turning more toward consumer protection. It includes regulations for more transparency to increase consumer awareness, prohibiting sale of few products or services to retail customers. There are new areas in which refined regulations are needed. These areas are arriving from regulatory developments of Fintech.

12.3.2 FINANCIAL ECOSYSTEM ACROSS GLOBE

The network of relationships with Fintech start-ups, governments, tech leaders, investors, regulators, media, and talent institutions together form Fintech ecosystem at international level. In global Fintech ecosystem, one firm's efforts in innovation help another to update their products/services. These Fintech firms will observe what others are doing and they will make same type of adjustments to their own products/services. Now the Fintechs are moving from competition to new collaborations for growth. Collaborations in the form of various types of partnerships, incubations, acquisition, etc., nationally or internationally. Although it is not an easy task as different countries have their own set of rules and regulations, culture and traditions in terms of size, efficiency, and acceptance. All the parts of Fintechs now have to pace with the race of technology at global level.

12.3.3 CONSUMER CONFIDENCE

It is very difficult to gain the confidence of consumers for Fintech services due to indulgence of cybercrimes at international level. Distrust arises from lack of knowledge and less understanding of services, absence of their physical locations, and the poor working of Fintechs. According to Wide Range Survey, London UK on 19th Oct 2018, 83% (8 out of 10 people) of UK consumers are unsure of Fintech services. This survey shows UK consumers do not trust on Fintechs and still feel comfortable with the services of traditional financial Institutions. To gain the confidence of consumers many Fintech firms offer the consumers simple and convenient financial services. Fintech has to educate/aware consumers to use their services in a safe manner. The Fintech marketers must concentrate mainly on conveying the advantages of their services in an effective way and from safety point of view rather than focusing on the promotion of their products only. There is a remarkable growth in Fintech international market past few years but lot more is still to be done to gain the confidence of consumers worldwide. For this, Fintechs have to deliver their message to consumers in a right manner.

12.3.4 LACK OF AWARENESS

According to the Global Fintech Adoption Index 2019 survey only 4% consumers across the globe are not even aware of money transfer. Overall 27% of respondent's priority is pricing over Fintech service and only 2% prefer to open account at ease. Lack of awareness is the biggest reason for low adoption rate of Fintech. Consumers do not know what products or services and options are available in the market. For this, social media is a good tool to provide information to consumers for their awareness from anywhere.

12.3.5 FINANCIAL INCLUSION

Financial Inclusion is a process to ensure access to financial products or services to weaker or low-income groups at very low or affordable prices in a transparent manner to meet their needs. It is a solution for developing or poor countries for their economic growth as the poor who are financially excluded earlier, will be now investing in business. It brings stability in their personal finance by saving for future. Financial Inclusion leads to digital finance usage. According to study conducted across 123 countries for checking the influence to own a saving account, by Allen et al. (2016) concluded that poor, low income, or illiterate person cannot benefit proportionately from financial inclusion in comparison to high income or educate person. This is very serious problem. Also there are some risks associated with Financial Inclusion such as risk of nonusability of digital devices, nonsuitability of products for low income, regulations, lack of good quality products, and high cost. The adoption is only when products are guaranteed to all and accessible to poor at low cost than to directly walk to Institute personally.

12.3.6 REGTECH AND SUPTECH

Regtech the short form of regulatory technology is bridging the gap between regulators and Fintechs. Regtech across the globe helps the Fintechs to comply with the norms with the uses of processes to prevent noncompliance, digitalization of data and improve risk management and reduced cost. Regtech provides fast and flexible solutions to meet these regulatory challenges which are also cost effective. According to a blog by Arun Suresh, about 10–15% of Fintech's workforce is engaged in regulatory compliance and analyst of Fintechs spends 90% of their time in collection and organization of data rather than analyzing. Regtech solutions made regulatory filing transparent and effective for firms. With the use of Regtech filing will become less time-consuming and analysts spend more time on analysis of data. While Suptech helped the regulatory agencies to digitalized data and automate regulatory procedures. Suptech ensures that there will be no gap in reporting process. It will reduce time and cost for collection of data and improves the scope of supervision. With Suptech regulator immediately receive a message on screen about violation through a customized monitoring system. This violation is based upon the parameters set up by regulatory authority. These regulations are set up differently according to the nature of Industry and financial habits and culture of respective country. Regtech and Suptech both internationally streamline and standardized workflows, introduce new capabilities and improve the efficiency of Fintechs. Through Fintech, Regtech, and Suptech new solutions will emerge that enables regulations to cope with the increasing complexity of supervision globally.

12.3.7 CYBERCRIME

Cyberattack is a serious issue for Fintech firms in fact it is a great challenge faced by Governments and organizations around the world. Cyberattacks are very sophisticated and frequent. One of the biggest challenges of Fintech firm is to keep data safe from these cybercrimes and to minimize the cyberattacks. With the emergence of Fintech most of the data is available digitally. Now the traditional cyber security methods are not effective. Fintech firms are reassessing the methods, adopting new technologies worldwide time to time while struggling to keep costs down. Cyber security has possible solution to the problem of cyberattacks globally. It includes data labeling and selective and identity aware data sharing. Now the mobiles and laptops equipped with biometric sensors are increasingly used for authentication through biometric, one time passwords, and code-generated authentication. This reduces dependence on traditional methods of PIN/Passwords which can be easily hacked. AI is a tool that is proactive or preventive and it discovers risks and prevents cyberattacks before its occurrence. Now AI becomes integral part of Fintech. Moving Target Defense is a new idea to improve cyber security. The method helps to reduce attacks. Moving Target Defense has deployed by US Department of Homeland Security already and by major European Banks.

12.3.8 DATA SECURITY AND PRIVACY RISK

In addition to cybercrime data security is also very important. Firms worldwide are gathering huge amount of data with the help of internet and mobile phone payment app services, which is used to analyze customer's buying patterns/behaviors, their strategies, and even their financial and personal information from anywhere across the globe. Protection of this data and providing it to different capacities in a very secure manner is very difficult for firms globally. Organizations seek permission from customers for data sharing, reuse and implement technologies to ensure them that data is not misused. Some of the main data security issues are data loss, insider threats; insecure API's, hijacking of accounts and shared vulnerabilities. Fintech firms also face privacy issues when it expands their services/ products from one jurisdiction to another jurisdiction with different rules. In 2017, some of the biggest US companies like Yahoo, Uber, and Equifax were attacked with cyberattacks. Even Yahoo has to pay $350 million as damages for the breach of security to customers.

12.3.9 BIG DATA USE

Big data consists of all data gathered by digital device, which will be analyzed to extract useful information about the consumers. This data is later used to learn customer's buying behavior, make strategies for financial institutes across the world. With this big data Fintechs easily modify their products or services to meet different customer's needs and even build new product or services according to international context to fit any country's customer needs. These customer profiles are also used to target market and attract new clients globally. Big data helps in fraud detection and risk management and provides personalized services internationally also.

12.3.10 AI USE

Fintechs are using AI for protection against frauds and threats. AI handles unstructured information regarding audio, visual, images, and location in a very effective way. There are AI solutions that are able to detect fraud and access risk management. The challenge that Fintechs are facing is to learn how to get benefits from AI without being attacked by cybercrime. AI's robots can help to decrease the risks by suggesting Fintech products and services from a huge amount of information.

12.3.11 CUSTOMER RETENTION

There is an increasing trend of managing money using various accounts/apps by customers. Opening too many accounts is due to customer's lack of trust. Nowadays customers around the globe are hedging against risks. If one account does not fulfill their requirements, it will be subside by the benefits of another. Fintechs are globally gaining market share but whether they can retain it or not, is the biggest challenge. Big Fintechs have experience of understanding consumer behavior and market so they attract newcomers and also they know what kind of retention policies is suitable. As the competition around the world is growing and new products are launching, making the customer retention very challenging for Fintechs worldwide.

12.3.12 SCALING

Fintech is facing very strict regulatory framework along with their problems of controlling cost, beating competition, and surviving in the market. As Sudhir Pai, CTO Financial Services Strategic Business Unit, Capgemini mentions, "Like most other sectors, Fintechs have realized that starting-up is relatively easy compared to scaling-up. Scaling-up requires particular strategies, approaches, and capabilities from the outset." Four Scaling up across border is a tough task, it includes navigation with local regulations, overcome with cultural and language barriers, and coping with limited resources and time. Only few Fintechs have managed to grow and gain profitability internationally. Most of the Fintech firms remove these across border barriers by collaborating their business in international market with existing players rather than competing with them. With these collaborations with the local players' risk of data breach, language problems, and any type of security issue can be eliminated hence building trust and reputation and scale their business successfully. One another secret of scaling up is to increase automation of routine interaction of customer. Fintech firms need to scale their payment system internationally also.

12.3.13 VOICE TECHNOLOGY

Voice Assistant being the part of AI, is being developed to handle Fintech services worldwide. This allows customers to have chat with Fintechs anywhere around the globe about the services and also helps the customers to calculate their amount of loan, planning for future, planning for savings, receiving updates of latest technologies, and searching for branches or ATMs. Call centers are the best example where direct call can be made quickly and easily. But there is still a lot of improvement that will be required.

12.4 CONCLUSIONS

Fintech globally aims to deliver financial services by making use of various softwares through modern technology like internet, smartphone, cryptocurrency, etc. Internationally Fintech also includes sectors and industries such as education, retail banking, fundraising, bitcoin, and investment management. Fintech is a platform where customers across the globe will get opportunities to choose from number of large options at competitive/affordable prices and even financial Institutions can improve with low costs. Fintech's demand is growing internationally day by day due to big digitally savvy companies seeking new technologies which provide convenience to use and better profitability. Fintech products help industries to attain cost efficiency and help business grow fast at international levels. New technologies like AI and Data-driven marketing will learn the habits of customer's spending and saving and their decisions in a better way. The AI technology helps the global customers with their works in an effective and speedy way and it keeps the staff cost low also. This technology brings certain problems also. All automation and digitalization process invites hackers who access the systems and steal all the information and misuse it. Governments across the world are facing difficulties to formulate uniform and standardized regulations globally and norms to protect consumers because of variety of different types of services provided by Fintech. There is still improvement that will be required.

KEYWORDS

- **initial coin offerings**
- **Insuretech**
- **Regtech**
- **Suptech**
- **cybercrime**

REFERENCES

3 Challenges of Scaling a Fintech Company across Borders on May 27, 2019 by Diego Caicedo. https://www.crowdfundinsider.com/2019/05/147779-3-challenges-of-scaling-a-fintech-company-across-borders/

5 Fintech Trends That Are Transforming Financial Services. https://www.cnbc.com/advertorial/2018/06/01/5-fintech-trends-that-are-transforming-financial-services.html

Blog by Ribhu S. on June 4, 2019. https://inc42.com/buzz/india-has-99-5-awareness-for-fintech-products-online-payments-ey-report/

Customer Retention for Financial Services in a Swipe Right Society by Steven Piper, June 19, 2019. https://sidigital.co/blog/customer-retention-financial-services

Das, S. Governor, Reserve Bank of India—March 25, 2019—Keynote Address Delivered at the NITI Aayog's FinTech. https://www.bis.org/review/r190325a.htm; https://m.rbi.org.in/Scripts/BS_SpeechesView.aspx?Id=1071

EY Global Fintech Adoption Index 2019 published on June 3, 2019. https://www.ey.com/en_us/news/2019/06/ey-global-fintech-adoption-index-finds-over- half-64-of-global-consumers-use-fintech; https://assets.ey.com/content/dam/ey-sites/ey-com/en_gl/topics/banking-and-capital-markets/ey-global-fintech-adoption-index.pdf

Financial Inclusion & Financial Literacy Bi OECD Seminar—Roundtable on the Updates on Financial Education and Inclusion Programmes in India by Dr. Deepali Pant Joshi, Chief General Manager-In-Charge, Reserve Bank of India. https://www.oecd.org/finance/financial-education/48303408.pdf

Financial Inclusion: Financial Inclusion Is a Key Enabler to Reducing Poverty and Boosting Prosperity. https://www.worldbank.org/en/topic/financialinclusion

Fintech and Its Challenges Article by Anuj Modi on April 6, 2019. http://www.businessworld.in/article/Fintech-And-Its-Challenges/06-04-2019-168786/

Fintech Ecosystem Playbook. https://www.ey.com/Publication/vwLUAssets/EY-fintech-ecosystem-playbook/$FILE/EY-fintech-ecosystem-playbook.pdf

FinTech, RegTech, and SupTech: A New Paradigm, Simultaneously Promoting Financial Service Innovation While Enhancing Supervisory Effectiveness, Published on March 21, 2018 by Franco Romanini. https://www.linkedin.com/pulse/fintech-regtech-suptech-new-paradigm-simultaneously-while-romanini-

How AI Technologies Help Banks and FinTech Startups by Vik Bogdanov/20 May 2019/Fintech. https://readwrite.com/2019/05/20/how-ai-technologies-help-banks-and-fintech-startups/

How Big Data Can Play An Essential Role in Fintech Evolution by Ryan Khan, July 24, 2018. https://www.smartdatacollective.com/fintech-big-data-play-role-financial-evolution/; https://thefintechtimes.com/how-to-implement-big-data-analytics-in-your-fintech-applications/

How Can Artificial Intelligence Help Fintech Companies. https://www.marutitech.com/how-can-artificial-intelligence-help-fintech companies/?

http://www.businessworld.in/article/Fintech-And-Its-Challenges/06-04-2019-168786/

https://datafloq.com/read/ai-fintech-should-we-be-concerned-cybersecurity/6184

https://info.currenciesdirect.com/gbfr_fintech

https://info.currenciesdirect.com/gbfr_fintech

https://www.globalbankingandfinance.com/the-three-biggest-fintech-challenges-facing-the-industry-right-now/

https://www.livemint.com/technology/tech-news/fintech-adoption-grew-64-in-2019-india-and-china-ahead-in-emerging-markets-ey-1559558964619.html

Lack of Awareness Means Canadians Are Lagging in Fintech by Clare O'Hara Wealth Management Reporter, Published January 31, 2016, Updated March

22, 2018. https://www.theglobeandmail.com/globe-investor/investment-ideas/lack-of-awareness-means-canadians-are-lagging-in-fintech/article28474152/

Major FinTech Cybersecurity, Data Security, and Privacy Protection Concerns by Terry Mansfield. https://medium.com/datadriveninvestor/major-fintech-cybersecurity-data-security-and-privacy-protection-concerns-51b401f5832a

Ozili, P. K.; Istanbul, B. Impact of Digital Finance on Financial Inclusion and Stability. *Review* **2018,** *18* (4), 329–340. https://www.sciencedirect.com/science/article/pii/S2214845017301503

Pai, S. CTO Financial Services Strategic Business Unit, Capgemini. https://gocardless.com/guides/posts/4-challenges-growing-fintech

RegTech: A New Disruption in the Financial Services Space by Arun Suresh. https://www.pwc.in/consulting/financial-services/fintech/fintech-insights/regtech-a-new-disruption-in-the-financial-services-space.html

Regulation and Supervision of Fintech—Ever expanding expectations; March 2019, kpmg.com. https://assets.kpmg/content/dam/kpmg/xx/pdf/2019/03/regulation-and-supervision-of-fintech.pdf

Review Article—Moving Target Defense Techniques: A Survey; by Lei, C.; Zhang, H-Q.; Tan, J-L.; Zhang, Y-C.; Liu, X-H. https://www.hindawi.com/journals/scn/2018/3759626/

Security Challenges in the Evolving Fintech Landscape Authored by Siddharth Vishwanath, Amol Bhat and Abhishek Chhonkar. https://www.pwc.in/assets/pdfs/consulting/cyber-security/banking/security-challenges-in-the-evolving-fintech-landscape.pdf

The Big Bang of Fintech , Regtech and Suptech; 16th July 2018 by Breana Patel, CEO, Thought Leader in Bank Risk and Regulations; Source: https://www.finextra.com/blogposting/15556/the-big-bang-of-fintech--regtech-and-suptech

The Cyber Security Challenges Facing Emerging Fintech Startups by Nick Ismail on April 17, 2018. https://www.information-age.com/cyber-security-challenges-emerging-fintech-startups-123471506/

What You Need to Know about the Fintech Ecosystem on March 29, 2016 by Centric Digital on Digital Trends. https://centricdigital.com/blog/digital-trends/what-you-need-to-know-about-fintech-ecosystem/

Wide-Ranging Survey, UK London, October 19, 2018. This Survey Was Carried Out by SurveyGoo and Studied the Attitudes of 2000 Consumers in the United Kingdom. https://www.realwire.com/releases/83-percent-of-UK-consumers-unsure-of-fintech-according-to-survey

Index

G